SELECTED PLAYS

SELECTED PLAYS

by

Tom Swift

Carysfort Press

A Carysfort Press Book in association with Peter Lang

Selected Plays
by Tom Swift

First published as a paperback in Ireland in 2012 by
Carysfort Press Ltd
58 Woodfield
Scholarstown Road
Dublin 16
Ireland

ISBN 978-1-78874-849-0

Typeset by Carysfort Press Ltd

eprint

This book is published with the financial assistance of
The Arts Council (An Chomhairle Ealaíon) Dublin, Ireland

Contents

for Jo

Acknowledgements

Many thanks to Lucina Russell and Kildare County Council Arts Office; Dan Farrelly, Eamonn Jordan, Lilian Chambers at Carysfort Press; Peter Crawley; Jim Culleton, Lynne Parker, Kevin Reynolds, Colm Hogan, Ciaran Bagnall, Margaret Hamilton, Brian Singleton, and everyone who made the publication of this book possible. Thank you also to all the performers, creative teams and production crews who brought these works to life.

List of Photographs

Introduction

by Peter Crawley

Some thirty years ago, Tom Swift awoke to discover that most of Dublin's population had disappeared. He was understandably surprised. In retrospect, the strange exodus had not come without warning. In recent days he had noticed the appearance of mysterious flags, now dangling in yellow and white from the windows of empty houses and closed shops. Swift cycled through the streets, as perplexed as The Omega Man while a short distance away, in the Phoenix Park, Pope John Paul II addressed a gathering of more than one million people, concluding, 'Young people of Ireland, I love you'.

The experience was not scarring, yet it lingers with the adult Swift still. Long before becoming a writer, he appreciated that a Church of Ireland upbringing made him a member of a minority, an outsider in his own country. Often he would encounter situations that made no sense. 'Thinking about it', he told me recently, 'it has to inform the way you see the world to an extent.'

Outsiders work well in theatre, which requires a slight remove, or a different angle, to transform the familiar into something fascinatingly strange. In part, Swift inherited that perspective from his father, a natural sceptic who warned his children not to take things at face value. It's a characteristic that informs other roles too: that of the journalist, the satirist and the revealing wit – all of which help to describe Tom Swift.

Some writers are born for the theatre, others arrive by invitation. Swift's first play, an adaptation of Voltaire's picaresque novel, *Candide*, was written at the request of Jo Mangan, who also co-wrote and directed the play. If the whirl of hardships, war and death in Voltaire's novella count as a withering assault against the doctrine of optimism (whose motto, "All is for the best in the best of all possible worlds," is left in tatters), the inaugural production of Performance Corporation in 2002 matched it with a playful aesthetic and endlessly inventive stagecraft. Each play in this collection was originally staged by the Performance Corporation and though Swift has explored different avenues ever since, such playfulness is a constant. The writing is precise, but leaves room for the discoveries of rehearsals, the flesh of the theatre. All plays are blueprints for performance, but several of these scripts – many of which are site-specific and all of them slyly topical – are documents for something unrepeatable.

It is hard to imagine *Dr Ledbetter's Experiment* (2004) conducted anywhere but Kilkenny, for instance. A promenade performance through the medieval city, it equips the audience with headphones and radio receivers to let us hear a 19th Century physician losing his mind. Time seems to soften and slip through the play, the text of words and thoughts gathering in layers, buffeted by anachronistic sound cues, to create a gentle disorientation. It is not quite madness (although we do hear voices) but it provides a shiver of Ledbetter's own gothic trajectory, torn between the *Book of Genesis* and *On the Origin of Species* as his worldview – like Candide's – is whipped out from under him.

For *Drive-By* (2006), Swift adapted the technology for a different purpose. Again the text is broadcast directly to the audience, blending live dialogue and recorded soundscapes. But this time we sit in cars watching boy racers whizz by, eavesdropping on verbatim interviews, stern newscasts and the staccato argot of petrol heads ('Keep her lit.'). Everything is juxtaposed, as though our radio dial is hopping. *Dr Ledbetter's Experiment* assigned the audience a new role with almost every scene – a history tour, a Church of Ireland congregation, errant schoolchildren or a prison committee. In *Drive-By* we belong, at times, to an accelerating subculture, a moralizing mass audience, or confidants to the personal tragedies of bereaved parents. Swift threaded journalistic enquiry into his narrative, aware that road deaths in Ireland attract more uninformed comment than investigation. Role-play, it seems, can be exhilarating, sobering and illuminating.

'It gets everywhere,' one character says of sand (and true love) in *Lizzie Lavelle and the Vanishing of Emlyclough* (2007). Indeed, it will swallow the fictitious town whole, as its two communities –

North and South – slip deeper into mutual enmity. Not even the metaphors of casual speech are safe. Lizzie, star player of the game of Ball for Emlyclough South, is 'purer than driven sand', insists her father. Michael, star player for Emlyclough North, would have 'seven shades of sand beaten out of him' by his fearsome mother were he to fall for a girl from the wrong side of the tracks. 'There's bad sand between us,' both sides agree. In that Swiftian ploy, clichés are exposed and subverted, and received language, ancient grudges and sectarian divides all seem inherently absurd. An archetypal story of sand crossed lovers, it shows – to borrow Philip Larkin's phrase – how misery deepens like a coastal shelf ('If you sink in the sand, I'll sink faster just to spite you!'). But in its thrumming good humour and the escape of its lovers to the bustling metropolis of Belmullet, it suggests that tragedy is not always inevitable.

On the face of it, *The Nose* (2008), Swift's adaptation of Nikolai Gogol's short story, and his business satire *Power Point* (2009) do not seem closely related. The first is a rare piece intended for a straight-ahead theatre space, based on a proto-absurdist Russian classic. The second is a site-specific piece, played out in the function room of a hotel or a business centre, whose source material – Guy de Maupassant's *Boule de Suif* – is buried so deep that a literary forensics specialist would struggle to find it. Both, however, are subtle, salient critiques of a nation in collapse, financially and morally.

Swift's version of *The Nose* – in which a Russian civil servant discovers not only that his nose has gone missing, but that it now outranks him – delights in oxymorons and slyly incongruous references. Major Kovalyev is wickedly undercut by his own preposterous sense of status ("Look, I am a self-made civil servant, so I'll be blunt.") while the poor but virtuous Olga has seen her dowry diminish in 'a stupid complex of luxury dachas'. For a contemporary Irish audience, whose own sense of status had begun its worrying descent, the 'unprecedented economic prosperity' of this whirligig vision of nineteenth century Russia seemed very close to home. It's not for nothing that Swift, who once worked as a television journalist, is at his most merciless when he sends up the meaningless patter of rolling media reportage, but for all his surreal frolics and pure comedy there is also a yearning for honesty. 'A fact is something that will stand up in a court of law,' points out one character, with a distinctly Hiberno-Russian grasp of irony, 'whereas the truth is ... tricky." Time and again authority figures are exposed as deceivers and mountebanks – conceited civil servants, careless doctors, fatuous news reporters, craven madams, even drunken barbers – but the play is not cynical. Its conclusion, and its restorative sense of decency, brings Swift's satire closer to Horace's ancient definition: to comment with a smile.

Where Maupassant chose to provoke, thrusting his reader into the moral expedience of French society with the exploitation and repudiation of a prostitute during the Franco-Prussian War, Swift's very loose adaptation of *Boule de Suif* enlists his audience as co-players in a parody of corporate culture, where values may plummet as well as rise. Attending a business seminar whose motivational excess is almost evangelical and jargonistic mantras spool out of our gurus Jack and Jill like a liturgy, in its own modest way the play anticipated the crumbling of Ireland's financial cathedrals and the bankruptcy of a nation. *Power Point*, though, works less like a narrative and more like a musical composition, from a galloping sardonic overture ('PANIC is the NUMBER ONE tool for SUCCESS in business today.') to incantatory recitations ('In the future the Internet will die ... unloved and alone in a bed-sit.') to a purging, wild finale. Having punctured the illogic of corporate cant, it finally seeks truth not in art, but unadorned reality, Swift's final unscripted scene letting the actors share genuine personal mementos and reminiscences. (In performance, director Jo Mangan injected some uncertainty: the photographs we were shown were blank.)

If that gesture suggested a conjuring trick – Swift as the disappearing writer – *Swampoodle* (2011) brought the idea further. A show *about* a show – which the audience may have just missed – it aims to tell the history of an Irish ghetto in Washington DC, paralleled with the declining fortunes of its performance space, the gargantuan, dilapidated Uline Arena. Once an historic venue, where the Ice-capades, Malcolm X and The Beatles all made appearances, it now boasts to be 'one of the city's premiere parking lots'. The American idioms and Irish voices here may be arch, but they also seem persuasive, unmediated speeches given by actors performing versions of themselves within a 'devised physical-slash-visual spectacle exploring the boundaries of what and how theatre can be'. That description staggers with self-reference and self send-up, but – as is the habit with Swift – it contains some truth. The playwright makes his own cameo here – as 'a clueless feckin' drunk' – as though Swift's anti-authoritarianism has now extended to himself, and through Shakespearean lifts and a frequent exhortation to seize the day he seems to be writing himself out of *Swampoodle*.

The play ends with the audience as writers of their own destiny, the real world beckoning them forth, waiting beyond a frame of parted curtains and fluttering jazz hands. We may be guided – through headphones, in cars, or along the freshly hacked trail of satire – but the experience of Tom Swift's theatre asks us to realize our own agency, to see things differently. Viewed from a slight remove, life seems more fresh, more comic, more honest. Or, as the cast of *Swampoodle* puts it, 'It's a wonderful show!'

Rory Nolan as Dr Ledbetter and Niamh Daly as Josephine
in Dr Ledbetter's Experiment.
Photo: Colm Hogan

Damien Devaney as Constable
in Dr Ledbetter's Experiment.
Photo: Colm Hogan

Tadhg Murphy as Boy 1, Ailish Symons as Girl and
Aidan Turner as Boy 2
in Drive-By.
Photo: Colm Hogan

Aidan Turner as Boy 2
in Drive-By.
Photo: Colm Hogan

Lisa Lambe as Lizzie
in Lizzie Lavelle and the Vanishing of Emlyclough.
Photo: Colm Hogan

Stephen Swift as Commentator
in Lizzie Lavelle and the Vanishing of Emlyclough.
Photo: Colm Hogan

Aonghus Óg McAnally as Major Kovalyev
in The Nose.
Photo: Ciaran Bagnall

Conan Sweeny as Katerina and Aongus Óg McAnally as Major Kovalyev in The Nose.
Photo: Ciaran Bagnall

Alan Howley as Jack and Clare Barrett as Mary
in Power Point.
Photo: Ciaran Bagnall

Lisa Lambe as Jill
in Power Point.
Photo: Ciaran Bagnall

Anastasia Wilson and Adrienne Nelson
in Swampoodle.
Photo: Ciaran Bagnall

Michael John Casey
in Swampoodle.
Photo: Ciaran Bagnall

DOCTOR LEDBETTER'S EXPERIMENT

AUTHOR'S NOTES

Locations

Dr Ledbetter's Experiment is a site-specific promenade work written for the Parliament Street area of Kilkenny City. The play begins in the lower medieval courtyard at Rothe House. The audience then moves to the upper courtyard, returns to the lower courtyard before being brought to the adjoining Gaelic League Hall. They then travel across the street to the Smithwicks Hall where a number of scenes are enacted. Finally, the audience walks along Parliament Street and into the City Gaol under Kilkenny City Courthouse.

Sound Design

At the start of the play, audience members are given personal headphones and an FM radio. During the play they listen to all the live dialogue, sound effects and original music through these headphones.

Recorded Dialogue

Where dialogue appears in brackets { } this denotes recorded dialogue, and is sometimes used to express a character's unspoken thoughts.

Doctor Ledbetter's Experiment premiered at the Kilkenny Arts Festival, August 2004. It was produced by The Performance Corporation and Kilkenny Arts Festival. In August 2006, the play was performed in the Edinburgh Festival Fringe as part of the Traverse Theatre programme.

Original Cast

Niamh Daly
Damien Devaney
Fergal McElherron
Aoife Molony
Rory Nolan.

Director: Jo Mangan
Sound Designer: Paul Brennan
Designer: Almha Roche
Lighting Designer: Kevin Treacy
Costume Designer: Suzanne Keogh
Composer: Rob Canning

SCENE 1

The lower courtyard of Rothe House, Kilkenny. The audience put on their headphones: They hear a quiet high-pitched tone, then the sound of the narrator's laboured breathing.

NARRATOR. It is peaceful here now. The walls and windows of Kilkenny show no signs of what went on here almost 150 years ago. The reflections in the windows, these stone walls which surround us, the very light of the sun itself yield no clues. But if you listen hard, you may hear echoes. They are memories or thoughts waiting to be released – waiting to be witnessed once more.

The sound of a light wind and the whisper of indecipherable voices.

Can you feel that? An echo from the shadows of a man who once traversed these streets: A good man, a bad man, a physician, a brute. What do you perceive?

Church bells, crowd sounds, tramping feet and the shout of a town crier.

TOWN CRIER. {Come see the blackguard Brennan meet his maker! Come see the blackguard Brennan meet his maker!}

Florence Ledbetter enters the lower courtyard.

FLORENCE. Saul! Saul! Hurry we shall miss it.

Dr. Saul Ledbetter follows, staring at his cupped hand.

LEDBETTER. Amaurobius Ferox! Is not the spider the most perfectly formed of God's creatures? I have this moment witnessed him pounce on his prey and drag it into his lair. He is all but blind and yet his remarkable sense of touch allows him to thrive in the darkness.

Lets the spider walk on his hand. The doctor becomes dreamy-eyed.

God's perfect creation. *[Produces a copy of Darwin's* On the origin of species*]* And yet this Dr Darwin would tell us that this spider has some prehistoric dragon as its ancestor.

LEDBETTER. {A man of science must maintain an open mind. Yet a Christian must denounce such ideas as blasphemy!}

He crushes the spider in his hand with a frown and throws it aside.

FLORENCE. *[Laughs]* Saul, I really wish you would not conduct your experiments in the public street. Now, please I wish to see the sentence announced.

LEDBETTER. I can tell you now he will be condemned to die. The poor know the taste of injustice only too well my dear. You know that I cannot and will not applaud the taking of another's life.

FLORENCE. Is it not plain to you – as it is to me – that this Private Brennan is the man who murdered those women and so he must pay the price. Even the novice at phrenology can see the man's features, the shape of his shaven skull are those of a murderer.

LEDBETTER. Phrenology? How can you believe such fables and fantasy? It is against reason.

FLORENCE. Saul. Come straight away. Let us see justice done.

Florence exits. Ledbetter stares after her.

LEDBETTER. {You bloodthirsty woman.}

Ledbetter reluctantly follows.

[To Audience] Yes that's right. Good people of Kilkenny. The entertainment lies this way. Can you not smell the hatred and fear? Justice is served at twelve noon, sharp.

SCENE 2

The audience follows Ledbetter into the upper courtyard. The sound of crowd chattering in excitedly. George Goodman and his wife Emily stand surveying proceedings. Ledbetter and Florence join them.

FLORENCE. My husband is too weak-willed to believe in justice. I say if he is guilty, he must pay for his sins. What do you believe, Uncle?

GOODMAN. Firing squad's too damn good for him, if you will excuse my French. Poor Florence you are not accustomed to such harsh language.

FLORENCE. *[Laughs]* You must think me deaf. I have heard such words before and much worse.

LEDBETTER. Mr Goodman, are you with the regiment in wishing to dispatch this bothersome matter quickly or do you celebrate with the Fenians in the death of one of the Queen's soldiers?

GOODMAN. Never quite knocked the Quaker zeal out of you, did I? Can't you see it's a practical matter? Separating the wheat from the chaff. *[Pause]* And Saul, I still expect my charge to show his guardian a modicum of respect.

LEDBETTER. What do you suppose the Lord Jesus Christ would have done if presented with a man like Brennan?

GOODMAN. Death by firing squad, I should imagine.

LEDBETTER. Do Florence and I not sit beside you at church each Sunday? Have I not heard you read the scriptures ...

GOODMAN. Eye for an eye, tooth for a tooth.

LEDBETTER. ... which tell us that forgiveness is the path of the righteous. Is not this faith in God's compassion, what makes us different from the beasts of the field, from the animals?

GOODMAN. My point precisely. The scoundrel's not human. He deserves to die.

A bugle call. A Colonel marches into the courtyard. The sound of the condemned man's breathing, then a drum roll.

COLONEL. A court martial of her majesty's army has tried this man, Private Ignatius Brennan ...

Angry shouts, the condemned man's breathing gets louder.

COLONEL. And found him to be guilty of the murders of Catherine Devine, Delia Fagan, May Sheflin, Rose Boylan and Mary Horsman. I hereby order that the sentence of death be carried out forthwith.

LEDBETTER. No! This sentence must not be carried out!

The crowd boos.

FLORENCE. Please Saul, not again. You cannot change the verdict.

Ledbetter leaps onto a boulder in the middle of the courtyard and turns to address the crowd.

LEDBETTER. This is against God's will! Only He *[raises hands up to heaven]* can sit in judgement.

The boos grow louder.

Please, listen. Only God, I tell you!

COLONEL. Doctor Ledbetter. Always the dissenter. I know this man to be guilty. I presided over the court martial which found him guilty as charged.

Crowd cheers.

LEDBETTER. Did not our Lord Jesus Christ preach the gospel of forgiveness? Even if this man were guilty of those crimes, the Christian, the moral, the human imperative demands that we should not take his life!

The condemned man's breathing and heartbeat gets louder.

COLONEL. Doctor Ledbetter. We all know you to be a friend of the poor and the sick but even the Good Samaritan would not dare to declare himself a proponent of murder.

The crowd boos. Ledbetter relents. He goes towards the lower courtyard, roughly dragging Florence with him.

LEDBETTER. I will not bear witness to this butchery. Animals! Animals!

GOODMAN. Ledbetter, leave her be!

COLONEL. Firing squad! Take aim! Fire!

Gunshots. The heartbeat stops. Rowdy cheers, mingled with the sound of wolves howling.

SCENE 3

The action freezes, and again the sounds of whistling wind and whispers are heard. In the distance, the screams of a woman. She pleads to be released.

NARRATOR. {Back and forth, back and forth they go, these echoes, bouncing from place to place through time. Did you hear that one? It might have been a forgotten thought, or an ancient nightmare, or a bad memory – One can never really tell. But don't let it upset you. Believe you me, these echoes often deceive and confuse.}

Florence confronts Ledbetter at the gateway leading to the lower courtyard.

FLORENCE. I simply fail to understand why you waste your breath on these lost causes. And why do you insist on humiliating yourself in the presence of the entire town?

LEDBETTER. Florence, if I must shout to uphold the sanctity of human life, I will do it. My father taught me: when a man holds a belief he must follow it to the last. When the great hunger came he fed the hungry and the sick till he too was a pauper and on his deathbed. His memory and the grief of his death are what inspire me. Mr Goodman was not so kind to his tenants.

FLORENCE. Without my uncle's charity you would be languishing in the poorhouse this very day. At least he takes good care of his own flesh and blood. You preach about morality, love, brotherhood and yet ...

LEDBETTER. And yet?

FLORENCE. Look within your own four walls. Look within! You confine yourself to your laboratory for days on end, doing I know not what. When you re-emerge your only concern is with rogues and murderers.

LEDBETTER. Have patience my love. I am very close now – close to a discovery which will change all our lives!

FLORENCE. More false promises!

Florence stares hard at Ledbetter.

FLORENCE. {Who are you? You are changing into a creature I no longer recognize.}

Florence exits, followed by Ledbetter. The Colonel ushers the audience through the gateway into the lower courtyard.

COLONEL. Come now, the day's business is done. God above will do with Private Brennan what He sees fit.

The audience moves to the lower courtyard to the sound of lowing cattle.

SCENE 4

In the lower courtyard, the whistling wind and whispers return. Nora, a young washer-woman appears on the balcony above with a bundle of white sheets. She hangs them up to dry. Ledbetter emerges from a doorway as a younger version of himself, sporting a boy's cloth cap. He is shy and diffident. He ascends the stairs to the balcony clutching a Church of Ireland prayer book. He coughs to attract attention.

NORA. Master Ledbetter. Have you come to pray for us or pray with us? Let's see. [Grabs prayer book] 'The Anglican Book of Common Prayer'. [Laughs] And Saul was blinded by a dazzling light! The glint off Goodman's shilling more likely. I suppose as long as he pays the bills, its fare thee well to the Quaker meetinghouse.

LEDBETTER. Nora, you know I had no choice.

NORA. The poor little orphan boy. Anyway what's with you? You're giving me the strangest look.

Throws the book back at him.

LEDBETTER. You know Nora. You know.

NORA. You want the washing back that I took from the house only this morning? Sure don't you know them heavy damasks take a day and a half to clean proper?

LEDBETTER. Stop. You know.

NORA. You've given the serving girls a day's rest and you're dropping off the dirty linen yourself?

LEDBETTER. Nora, I know it is a sin. I cannot help it ... I have money.

NORA. Well there's a new one for you. And there was me thinking Mr Goodman's paying to send you to medical school above in Dublin with pissybed seeds.

LEDBETTER. Please.

NORA. Money you say?

Nora beckons him to enter.

Let's have a look at what class of money you're talking about young Saul Ledbetter. But I'm telling you this is the last time, this week.

They disappear behind the hanging sheets to the sound of monkeys chattering and screaming.

SCENE 5

The Reverend Spencer – an elderly man – emerges from the door of the Gaelic League Hall on the upper side of the courtyard. Inside is a Church of Ireland chapel.

SPENCER. Please come in. You are all so very welcome. I am always gratified to welcome new parishioners to our little church.

The Reverend Spencer hands out hymn books to the audience who sit in the church's pews. Opposite are seated Goodman and Emily. Ledbetter enters out of breath and gets a withering stare from Goodman.

Please be seated. We shall be commencing the service shortly. If you open your hymnbooks we will start with number 357.

The congregation and audience sing 'All Things Bright and Beautiful'.

All things bright and beautiful. *[Sighs]* Thank you for joining us as we pray to our Lord Jesus Christ. *[Pause]* Dear Lord, You created the world, heaven and earth. Lord thank you for all the bright and beautiful gifts of nature you have given us. Amen.

CONGREGATION. Amen.

SPENCER. Beautiful.

He loses himself in religious reverie. Goodman coughs. Spencer comes to, not realising he's been daydreaming.

And now we shall have a reading from the book of Genesis. Doctor Ledbetter?

Ledbetter walks to the lectern and opens the Bible.

LEDBETTER. And God made the beast of the earth after his kind, and cattle after his kind, and every thing that creepeth upon the earth after his kind: and God saw that it was good. And God said, Let us make man in our image, after our likeness: and let them have dominion over the fish of the sea, and over the fowl of the air, and over the cattle, and over all the earth, and over every creeping thing that creepeth upon the earth. This is the word of the Lord.

CONGREGATION. Amen

Ledbetter stares at the congregation. He holds up Darwin's On the Origin of Species.

LEDBETTER. This is the word of the Lord ... But be warned. There is another book, which would have us believe an immoral story of creatures that crawled from the mud, millions of years past. Dr Darwin's *On the origin of Species* tells us that from the loins of some of these creatures came forth the line of mammals; from others of their kin came forth the fowl of the air and so on.

The sounds of the jungle ... The congregation begin to act in an ape-like manner. Emily picks a nit out of Goodman's hair. Reverend Spencer scratches his head. Ledbetter rubs his eyes in disbelief. The congregants return to their normal human form.

And what is more, if you were to read this hateful pamphlet, and I have read it many times, you can only conclude that men are nothing more than first cousins of monkeys! Imagine brethren, the horror this implies. If we are beasts should we not treat our fellow man as we do animals? Should we not scourge them, enslave them, and slaughter them without remorse or pity. That is why I say to you reject this book. It is a Pandora's box of lies and horror!

Silence. Ledbetter appears flustered as if he's suddenly snapped out of a dream and meekly returns to his seat.

SPENCER. Lovely. May the Lord protect you and keep you, may he guide you and comfort you from this day forth. Go in peace. Amen.

CONGREGATION. Amen.

The congregation shuffles out apart from Goodman and Ledbetter.

GOODMAN. Shameful, simply shameful. Have you forgotten? You are a medical doctor not a preacher. And as for this ranting about Darwin – you protest too much about this Godless theory which has already been disproved. I told you before, do not dabble in science and theorizing! And if you persist in making a fool out of me I shall cut you off without a penny.

LEDBETTER. I confess I do not know what possessed me, Mr Goodman. I am a little tired of late. My seclusion in the laboratory has had an odd effect.

Goodman smiles weakly, looks about, then offers Ledbetter a pinch of snuff.

GOODMAN. Here, have some. Emily abhors this stuff.

Ledbetter refuses. Goodman takes a sniff, sneezes once very politely but is then wracked by a massive sneezing fit. His gestures and sneezes become animal-like as he writhes about. Ledbetter looks on in horror.

LEDBETTER. Mr Goodman. Mr Goodman. Stop that. Please stop.

Goodman staggers out of the chapel still wracked by the seizure. Ledbetter follows.

Please, Mr Goodman!

SCENE 6

A whistling wind and whispers ... A schoolmistress in 1920's clothing enters and beckons the audience to follow her.

MISTRESS. Children hurry up! We must make haste to the schoolhouse for scripture lessons. Please children this way.

She beckons the audience out into the lower courtyard and onto Parliament Street. The sound of horses and the cries of street sellers.

As your headmistress I expect and demand your attention and obedience at all times. Now children it's time to cross the road.

The schoolmistress holds the traffic on Parliament Street to allow the audience to cross. She leads them towards the Smithwicks Hall.

Careful! Please pay attention to the horses – They are liable to bolt at a moment's notice. Quickly now, I trust your parents told you that the black and tans have left Kilkenny barracks. If they don't get you, then the IRA men will. Henry? Where is Henry, children? Quick children, get inside. But you must have seen him. Oh my dear Lord, you must have seen him.

As the audience enters the Smithwicks Hall the soundscape changes from 1920's street sounds to the noise of a jungle teeming with wildlife. The Schoolmistress wanders slowly into the darkness muttering a mantra.

You must have seen him. You must have seen him. You must have seen him ...

NARRATOR. {Fascinating. As I told you, our friends the echoes are prone to fragment, confuse, ricochet. This is no schoolhouse. We have arrived in a different place altogether. Now quickly stand over there. Yes there where I can see you. Hurry up. Shush, now. Listen or the echoes will become distorted.}

SCENE 7

The smash of breaking glass. The lights go up on the doctor's lab. Ledbetter is holding the neck of a broken lab container in one hand and inhaling deeply from a smoking beaker in the other. He's trembling. Behind him are three cages from which comes the squeaking of small animals. He turns to the cages and violently prods the animals with a metal spike. The animals cry in pain. Satisfied, the doctor sits down to write a letter.

LEDBETTER. {Dear Dr Darwin, I trust you have received my previous epistles and await your reply. I recently read with great shock your work 'On the origin of species'. Your thesis has at its core, an assumption that ... }

Ledbetter looks up.

... God himself does not exist! *[Pause]* I refer you to the book of Genesis and challenge you to find a single reference to 'natural selection' or indeed 'survival of the fittest'. *[Pause]* On another matter, I am pleased to tell you I am conducting my own research.

A maid, Josephine, enters unseen by Ledbetter with a teapot on a tray.

My thesis does not propose that the creatures evolve into some other species as you do. *[Impassioned]* Rather, my experiments have found that ... Josephine, I did not see you. I have taken to writing aloud, if you understand.

Ledbetter continues writing. She gently places the tray on his desk, her gaze fixed on him.

JOSEPHINE. No forgive me, sir. I'll be going now, sir.

Ledbetter continues writing. Josephine backs away. She picks up a shard from the broken beaker, hesitates and then cuts her hand. She gasps in pain and the doctor leaps to her side.

LEDBETTER. Quick, hold it like so.

JOSEPHINE. I am so sorry sir.

Ledbetter holds her wrist roughly and wraps a bandage around her hand. He tries to avoid her stare.

LEDBETTER. Now that should be right as rain in no time.

JOSEPHINE. Is it the lines on my face sir?

LEDBETTER. Yes, right as rain.

JOSEPHINE. Sir, is that what it is? Is that why you cannot look me in the face?

LEDBETTER. I think you should retire for the evening, Josephine. You are distressed but I assure you the lesion is not deep.

She grabs Ledbetter's wrist with her free hand

JOSEPHINE. It hurts sir. Why should it be impossible for two people, such as we are, to be... I know you are a married respectable gentleman and *[Bitter]* you love your wife. But was I not always discreet? You were happy with me once ...

JOSEPHINE. { ... happy to whisper your affections in my little ear, happy to lie with me.}

She lets go and begins peering into the animal cages.

I know my face has grown freckled and lined. But a poor girl has no choice. Work and worry; the sun and rain take care of that. Did you not tell me this miraculous cure you were concocting to treat those poor creatures you torment day and night. You told me you were the man who was going to 'turn back the very hands of time'.

Ledbetter backs away as she moves closer.

Why not make a little guinea pig of me? I won't bite.

LEDBETTER. *[annoyed]* I cannot recall any of this Josephine. As I said, you are upset.

JOSEPHINE. It's you will be upset when Mrs Ledbetter finds out what you've been up to with Nora the washerwoman's daughter! That'll set the queen bee in a tizzy!

Ledbetter raises his hand to strike her but stops himself. Josephine stumbles backwards in fright, then exits.

LEDBETTER. Forgive me Josephine, please.

Ledbetter takes another drag from the mysterious smoking beaker. Darkness falls.

SCENE 8

A light wind and whispers followed by the muffled sound of 1970's music.

NARRATOR. {Forgive me. There has been some interference. I assure you this has nothing whatsoever to do with me.}

In another part of the space, a young man in dishevelled clothes is chained to the wall. He's blindfolded and gagged. He rocks back and forth in a distressed state. The sound of a fuzzy and intermittent radio broadcast ...

NEWSREADER. { ... has been the driest summer on record. *[Pause]* The Garda Commissioner ... was no link ... unsolved disappearances ... all went missing during ... County Kilkenny ... families are demanding a new investigation....}

The light fades further. A dark figure approaches the young man and overshadows him. The young man lets out a muffled scream. Darkness.

SCENE 9

Ledbetter inhales from a smoking beaker in his lab before staggering to a dining table where Florence waits for him. A large silver dome sits on the table. A piano sonata plays somewhere in the distance.

FLORENCE. Saul, why is there no place set for you? You have spent two days in the laboratory with barely a scrap of food. Why can you not tell me what you do in that odious chamber? Saul, are you listening?

LEDBETTER. Yes.

FLORENCE. I do wish you would listen. Did I tell you I received a letter from Dublin this morning, from mother?

LEDBETTER. Precisely.

FLORENCE. Listen. She writes, 'The gardens at Fitzwilliam are more delightful than ever. I noted on my last visit to Kilkenny that your gardens have fallen into a state of disrepair that reminded your father of Borneo. You really should employ a more dedicated gardener...

LEDBETTER. I see.

FLORENCE. She intends to visit soon.

LEDBETTER. Exactly.

Florence leaps abruptly to her feet and begins to gesticulate.

FLORENCE. You realise I will not be here to entertain her. I will have escaped to Dublin to join the chorus at the Royal Theatre. *[Raises her dress provocatively]* Every night I shall tease the footlights with a glimpse of petticoat. And no doubt I shall adjourn to a convenient opium house at the close of each performance where I will enjoy the company of burly stevedores and Chinese sailors ...

[pause] Saul? Saul! Do you know who I am? Please. I am not a dog lying in your path to be stepped over – I am your Florence.

Ledbetter stares vacantly at Florence. There's a knock at the door, and Josephine enters out of breath.

JOSEPHINE. Dr Ledbetter, Mrs Ledbetter. My mother has taken very badly ill again. She calls for you doctor. Please come, sir.

FLORENCE. The doctor and I are having dinner. I will not have the servants intrude in such a manner.

LEDBETTER. Josephine, I will attend to your mother as soon as I can.

Josephine exits.

FLORENCE. She is ill so often, it is a miracle of medicine that this girl's mother continues to live at all. You think I am blind to this charade but I am not. You will not go, I command you!

LEDBETTER. The woman needs medical attention. You do not command me. You are duty bound to love, honour and obey me.

Josephine appears in the shadows, eavesdropping.

FLORENCE. Ha! Love and honour – the very things you would give to all but me. Don't think I haven't noticed how nicely you bandaged Josephine's little hand.

LEDBETTER. Quiet I say! You will obey me!

Ledbetter grabs a carving knife from the table and holds the blade to Florence's neck.

FLORENCE. Cut away, cut away. What difference will it make? I am already dead to you!{Return to me my love. Look at me.}

LEDBETTER. Stop this blasphemy!

Ledbetter lowers the knife.Florence throws back her head revealing more of her bare neck. Ledbetter trembles with anger and raises the knife to her throat again.

Perhaps, I should do it! At least then I would be rid of your tormenting ways!

Ledbetter drops the knife to the floor and slumps back into his chair.

LEDBETTER. A darkness has fallen over me Florence. A darkness in which I cannot sense the way to go – I have prayed to God to show me the path but he does not answer. I cannot tell if I am dreaming or awake and you are the one thing that tethers me to reality. All I see about me is disease, cruelty and death. Do I commit a sin if I try to end that suffering?

Josephine emerges from the shadows, smiling and reaching towards Ledbetter.

Get out! Go away!

SCENE 10

The sound of clanking engines, steam-powered machines and the excited murmur of a lecture hall. Dr Jenkins – an elderly English professor – enters and stands in the midst of the audience.

JENKINS. Gentlemen, as chairman of the Linnean Society it is my pleasure to welcome Dr Saul Ledbetter, the renowned Irish scientist here to London to address us. Gentlemen, Dr Ledbetter has for some time now been investigating the causes and effects of the ageing process upon the 'Corpus Humana'. He is confident you will be amazed by his findings.

Ledbetter takes centre stage.

LEDBETTER. Gentlemen, I put to you this evening the proposition that human life is not a finite process.

Murmurs of disbelief from the Linnean Society members.

It astounds you but it is true. Death is by no means a certainty. I tell you now – we have it in our power to turn back the ever-ticking clock of man's mortality ... by returning the body to womb itself!

Gasps of amazement.

It is universally accepted that within the womb the seed of human life thrives as at no other time. And what of the conditions in which this miracle occurs? You will agree that in this cocoon the growing child is denied light, denied sound, denied food in the sense that we understand it. He is in a state of what I term 'Sensory Denial'. This led me to ponder the possible effects on my laboratory animals if I were to recreate the conditions which foster life itself! For weeks on end, confined in darkened cages, I denied these animals all the normal sensory stimulations. The cages were proofed against sound, their food was minimal and they were administered a particular ... medication to dull the sense of touch.

JENKINS. Surely, Dr Ledbetter, this is an inhumane treatment.

LEDBETTER. May I remind you, Dr Jenkins, that these tests were conducted on mere animals. Their lives are of little consequence when weighed against mankind's advancement. I grant you, those few that did survive appeared greatly disturbed, and yet ... And yet these animals had undergone an undeniable physiological metamorphosis. They entered those cages as normal fully grown adults. They re-emerged younger, stronger, more virile than before – Gentleman they had reverted to their juvenile state! I had turned back the clock!

LINNEANS. {Outrageous! Charlatan! Show us your proof, sir. Show us your proof.}

LEDBETTER. Gentlemen, please! With this finding, we shall overcome sickness and infirmity forever!

Goodman enters in an enraged state.

GOODMAN. Saul! What the Dickens are you doing, you beast?

LEDBETTER. Can you not see that I am engaged in a lecture?

GOODMAN. Have you been mesmerised man? Look at you, chattering away to yourself like a baboon. You will hang for this, I tell you you will hang on high!

LEDBETTER. Mr Goodman?

GOODMAN. You'll be sorry to hear that your wife was still alive – Still breathing when they found her in a pool of her own blood. Your name was all she uttered – your name Saul.

Ledbetter staggers on his feet.

You will come with me. I'll see to it that the constabulary beat you till you confess.

Goodman leads Ledbetter out in a confused state.

SCENE 11

A light wind and whispers, then a rumbling ominous sound as if we are deep underground. Fluorescent lights flicker on. A man is standing on a chair, his arms in cruciform. His wrists are tied with ropes to the roof beams above. The prisoner wears dishevelled modern clothes. He is scared and squints out into the darkness.

INTERROGATOR. Do we look like total fools? Just tell us what you did with the girl.

PRISONER. I keep telling you ... It wasn't me ... It was him ... Tricked the both of us ... Told us lies ... And when we got there it was so dark ... Couldn't see the hand in front of your face and ... I was losing my mind trapped in there – the place was full of animals – they wouldn't leave me alone.

INTERROGATOR. Losing your mind. Yeah. Good description.

PRISONER. What? What?

INTERROGATOR. Lost his sense of hearing and all.

PRISONER. It wasn't me. *He* tricked us.

INTERROGATOR. This fairytale again! You were the last one seen with her, you turn up weeks later, in this state, with no sign of the girl. And you can't even give a description of this 'zookeeper'.

PRISONER. It's the truth!

INTERROGATOR. I know your sort. You really don't deserve this – to have me asking you this and asking you that; begging you – tell me what happened, tell me the truth. Because you don't hear me, and you don't understand.

The interrogator kicks the chair rhythmically. The prisoner panics trying to maintain a foothold.

You're on a lower level. You're a dumb, sick animal. And there's only one language animals understand.

The lights flicker and go out. The prisoner screams as we hear him being savagely beaten. This is suddenly interrupted by radio interference.

SCENE 12

Funereal music and the distant rumble of thunder. Goodman and Emily stand around uneasily in the parlour of the Ledbetter house. Ledbetter sits apart from them. He has changed physically. He is stooped and bruised about the face.

LEDBETTER. {Behold, thou hast driven me out this day from the face of the earth; and from thy face shall I be hid; and I shall be a fugitive and a vagabond in the earth. *[Pause]* I see the way you regard me. You do not see the man who healed and tended you – you see a monster.}

Laughs bitterly to himself drawing stares from the mourners.

GOODMAN. *[Whispers]* I raised a viper! The very sight of his false tears makes my blood boil.

EMILY. George dear, please. Won't you let him grieve? Saul was questioned. That is all. He has been charged with nothing.

GOODMAN. He's the man all right. They simply did not beat him enough.

Reverend Spencer enters and commiserates with the Goodmans and then with Doctor Ledbetter.

LEDBETTER. Tell me this Reverend, if God is love then why should he choose to destroy love, and put in its place pain and anger? He has taken her from me just as He ripped my mother and father from me when I was a boy. I am no Job! Why does He test me thus?

GOODMAN. Do you question God's will sir?

The thunder gets louder.

SPENCER. No please Mr Goodman, he is upset. Do not vex him further.

GOODMAN. Do you question God sir?

LEDBETTER. Yes I do question him, sir. Every night I pray to him – imploring him to tell me why men act like beasts, why the strong dominate the sick and the weak, why the rich enslave the poor and why they cast out those who speak the truth. I question Him, but my only reply is the echo of my own voice; an empty echo!

There's a crash of thunder and a blinding flash of lightning. In unison, the mourners crouch in fear. They take on the form of cowering apes, then slowly 'evolve' back to their upright human form. Ledbetter is transfixed. He takes a copy of Darwin's book from his pocket. He flicks manically through the book to a marked page. He stares in amazement at the book, then at the mourners and then back at the book. A slow smile of understanding creeps across his face. Blackout.

SCENE 13

A sudden loud knocking on a heavy door, and then more frantic knocking, as if someone is trying to escape. A big wooden door creaks open and we hear coughing and moaning.

VOICES. {Please Doctor, please Doctor. For the love of God, she's dying – will you not help. Please Doctor will you cure her, please.}

Ledbetter is in his lab. He looks ill and his body seems wracked with pain. He is inhaling from a glass beaker, while staring wide eyed at a pair of scissors in his other hand. He puts down the beaker and slips the scissors in his pocket. The sound of circus music. Suddenly the doctor adopts a showman persona. Josephine enters. Ledbetter twirls her around.

LEDBETTER. Enter! Enter the sick and the lame and the leper! Who am I, you ask? I am one of you. Come and be healed. Place your trust in me and together we shall evolve to a new state of well-being. Welcome to the Ledbetter Infirmary!

An old woman and her timid adult son enter. Josephine greets them with a flourish of mock ceremony.

JOSEPHINE. Sir, Madame, come this way. You seem quite sprightly. What is it that ails you?

MR KEOHANE. No it's not for me ma'am that I've come. My old mother is the one who is full of old maladies and ...

MRS KEOHANE. I'm 76!

JOSEPHINE. Well then, you need urgent attention, don't you? What exactly ails you ma'am?

MRS KEOHANE. I'm old and wrinkled and my bones ache with the years. Is that not enough, girl?

MR KEOHANE. Up and down Parliament Street they're all talking about the doctor's healing gift. Is it ... Is it true?

MRS KEOHANE. Is it for free the fool wants to ask! Well? How much is it, girl?

LEDBETTER. Here, no one pays a penny. I embrace the poor and the sick – and reject the rich, as they have rejected me. Josephine please tend to the lady.

Josephine leads her away with a wicked smile. Ledbetter circles Mr Keohane, looking him up and down.

Sir. You are ill.

MR KEOHANE. I am?

LEDBETTER. The outward manifestations are only perceptible to a trained eye but you are a very sick young man and in need of immediate treatment. The ravages of age are already apparent on your face.

MR KEOHANE. But, but ... Mr Tehan will be looking for me back at the shop. If I'm late...

LEDBETTER. Don't worry my boy. You will be eternally grateful to me when the job is done. Josephine direct him to the anteroom – And Josephine I wish to speak with you.

JOSEPHINE. Doctor Ledbetter, this man does not need treatment. You burden yourself with too much work.

LEDBETTER. He shall undergo a new type of treatment. It is a process only the healthy and the deserving can withstand. Do you deserve it, Josephine? You told me once you wished to be my guinea pig. Is that still your desire? You said you loved me, that you would do anything for me.

JOSEPHINE. Saul?

Ledbetter advances on Josephine.

LEDBETTER. You loved me so much that you plunged a pair of scissors *[Produces scissors]* into the breast of my beloved wife and watched life drain from her body. If you love me that much then you will do what I ask. You will submit to my experiment. Yes, there will be pain and yes, you will cry out to God himself for mercy. But you will get no reply.

Ledbetter grabs Josephine by the wrists and drags her away.

SCENE 14

Ledbetter's lab is in disarray. It looks as if it is covered with a layer of dust. A dour middle-aged man, the coroner, enters. He walks about the lab taking notes and occasionally inspecting its contents through a magnifying glass. He turns to address the audience.

CORONER. It is the finding of this coroner's inquest that the nine souls who perished in the house of Dr Saul Ledbetter died from starvation, unsanitary conditions and opiate consumption during periods of incarceration of up to six months. May the Doctor spend 20 times as long rotting in jail for his crimes!

Picks up a letter from the writing desk and examines it.

I shall read this into the record of my report. It is dated August of last year. Dear Dr Darwin, The experiment continues successfully and it is now 5 months since the volunteers first entered their cubicles. I confess, they complain daily about their conditions but it was they who demanded a cure, for man's greatest sickness – the ageing process itself. I remind my patients – or as I call them my pets – that I am duty bound to administer the full course of sensory denial and feel certain they will thank me in the end. Unfettered as I now am by the fables of Christian thinking I feel, for the first time, a true man of science and my research has become an end in itself. Having tested the treatment myself, I have concluded that the process cannot and should not benefit all the patients. Some have become weak and may not stand the test. It is indeed the process of Natural Selection at work in my own laboratory.

The coroner drops the letter in disgust.

Kind Regards, Your Faithful Servant, Dr Saul Ledbetter. Take the survivors hence from this terrible darkness. Take them into the light!

SCENE 15

The door of the Smithwicks Hall bursts open, letting in the light. We hear a light wind and whispers. A nervous-looking police constable in an early 20th century uniform beckons the audience to the exit door. The constable leads them along Parliament Street. He speaks only in whispers and tiptoes so as not to step on the cracks in the pavement.

CONSTABLE. Ladies and gents of the prison reform visiting committee, you might like to take a moment to compose yourselves for I know your visit to the house of the villain Ledbetter will have caused severe upset to you – especially the ladies. You know, it's thirty years to the day since his torture chambers were discovered but those who visit the place still swear they hear echoes from its wicked past. We mustn't linger any longer, as you'll want to inspect the place where Ledbetter remains imprisoned for those crimes.

The constable arrives at the door of the Gaol. He seems to shake with fear.

Now, I know the committee has seen many hellish gaols in its time but I'd say even you are a small bit nervous about this one, given its reputation. Of course I am used to it, so it doesn't take a feather out of me, not a feather. There was a time when I'd be shaking like a leaf before entering the dungeons, I mean the city gaol as it's more properly called, but not anymore, oh no. Right so, here we are, the gates o' hell – sorry ladies, a very poor jest. Stand back now, stand back!

The constable heaves the door of the gaol open with a massive creak. The sound of moans emanates from within. The constable enters the darkness of the gaol and beckons the audience to follow him.

SCENE 16

CONSTABLE. Welcome to the home of Dr Saul Ledbetter. The inspection won't take too long as he's the only prisoner left in here. Got the run of the place *[laughs nervously]* and so there's no need for more than just the one gaoler.

Ominous creaks and distant moans.

[Whispers] Mr Hughes? Mr Hughes! Please follow me, follow me. But don't step on the cracks, don't step on the cracks, don't step on the cracks.

He beckons the audience to follow him down the gloomy central corridor of the gaol. His voice starts to distort, then he vanishes from sight. The door of the gaol slams shut with a bang.

HUGHES. I'm here, I'm here – over here behind you.

Hughes – a pale stooped man in disheveled clothing – appears from behind the audience. He carries a lantern and a stool. He hops up on the stool.

I wasn't expecting you this early, but sure we'll make the most of it. I have totally lost track of the time and you people will want to be getting on, isn't that right. Of course it is. Busy people. I'm terribly sorry. *[Shakes his pocket watch]* What time is it? This thing is broken. You get terrible lost without the watch, don't you? Of course you do. Sure at this stage I wouldn't even know what year it is – Could be the 23rd century for all I know. Well listen, I won't keep you. We must press on. Come this way.

He turns and starts off down the corridor. Then stops suddenly and turns to face the audience.

Stop! Listen. Don't you love the silence of it all? Of course you do. No listen hard.

VOICES. {Help, let me out. Please let me out!}

HUGHES Silence is golden, isn't it? You heard something? Nonsense, that does not make the slightest bit of sense. There's nothing to see, nothing to hear, nothing to ... It's all in your head. Take a look around. It's all in your head. Take a look around...

Hughes bows, then retreats, backwards down the corridor, bowing all the while. As he does so he points with a flourish to each cell door he passes.

Take a look around. That's what you're here for, isn't it?

VOICES. { ... and she was such a beautiful girl, so beautiful. Cathy if you can hear this, we love you ... He always kept in touch, he was such a good lad, such a good lad...You can never give up hope, you know. You've got to keep looking ... and her coat was still hanging under the stairs and you could smell the scent she used to wear (*starts crying*) ... of course I'm bitter. I'll never see him again. That bitter taste never goes away. It lasts forever. }

Through peepholes in the cell doors the audience see a series of bizarre installations. In one cell baby dolls hang from the ceiling bathed in red light. On the door of another cell we see a looped film projection of a woman posing with her grandchild outside a terraced house. In one cell there appears to be someone inside. All we can see when we peer through the hatch is a staring eye. In one of the corridors off the main area a woman in Victorian dress wears a leather mask covering her entire head. She rocks back and forth groping in the dark. We hear a light wind and whispers. As if from nowhere Hughes again appears, frantically checking his broken watch.

HUGHES. Has anyone got the time? Do you know I've completely lost track. Well at least tell me what year it is?

He elicits an answer from an audience member.

What?! No, that doesn't make a blind bit of sense. I've kept you here too long, haven't I? Of course I have, too long entirely. And you haven't even seen himself. Come follow me.

Hughes frantically beckons the audience to follow. Hughes peeps into a cell and reels back in shock.

Eek! He promised me. He did now, honest he did. He said it wouldn't happen this ... Ladies and gents there's been an ... irregularity. Please, now we've no time to lose. Ladies and gents, for your own safety, you come with me this way. Into the cell!

Hughes ushers the audience into a cell which is dark apart from a small light illuminating a hanging doll in the corner. The door is slammed shut. Hughes is visible through the cell door hatch, outside the door. We hear the narrator's laboured rasping voice – this time he seems to be close by.

NARRATOR. I thought I heard an echo, I was sure I heard an echo. Was it vanity or curiosity that brought you here? No matter, after so many years I cease to ask questions. Those before you sought what fools have always craved – eternal youth. They were the ones least equipped to stand the test.

A light gradually illuminates the speaker. It is the stooped figure of Doctor Ledbetter standing on a ledge above the audience.

I have survived because I am a man of science. I entered this without selfish pretensions. I do this for the benefit of all mankind – so perhaps one day we may suffer death and disease no more. My adaptation under conditions of sensory denial – my evolution if you will – surprised even me. Imagine, eighty years, then one hundred, then one hundred and forty years added to the natural lifespan of the human animal. How they mocked when I said human life is not a finite process. I can tell that you do not come here to mock, you are here to learn. You are here to offer yourselves to science – to pursue an ideal, whatever the pain, whatever the price.

Hughes shuts the cell door hatch with a bang.

Thank you Hughes. I note you have already given my volunteers their hearing deprivation devices – an excellent way to commence the process of gradual and complete sensory denial.

Ledbetter leaps off the ledge towards the audience. As he does so, the cell is plunged into total darkness. He rushes out of the cell, slamming the door shut. He peers through the hatch.

Now my pets, remember, some of you will evolve and be strengthened by the experiment – but the weak will perish. Do not fear – it is an unfortunate but unavoidable process – what Dr Darwin would call 'survival of the fittest'.

The audience is left in complete darkness. The sound of shrieking monkeys is all that remains.

DRIVE-BY

Author's Note

Drive-By is an outdoor site-specific work written for the R and H Hall silo yard in Cork docks. Before the play commences, the audience park their cars facing the yard. A road or 'runway' passes through the space. The audience watch the performance from their vehicles. All of the play's dialogue, music and sound effects are transmitted to the audience's car radios.

Drive-By premiered at the Cork Midsummer Festival, June 2006. The play was co-produced by The Performance Corporation and Once-Off Productions. In October 2007, the play was performed as part of The Canterbury Festival, England.

Original Cast

Boy 1: Tadhg Murphy
Boy 2: Aidan Turner
Girl: Ailish Symons

Director: Jo Mangan
Lighting Designer: Arno Nauwels
Costume Designer: Suzanne Keogh
Sound Designer: Tom Swift
Stunt Director: Donal O'Farrell

The R and H Hall yard, Cork city docks. The audience park their cars around the edge of the yard. Three cars covered with sheets are parked facing the audience's cars. A thumping techno track plays, interspersed with sound-bites from recordings of real boy racers as well as sound effects of jets screaming overhead, an ambulance and a car crash. Boy 2 struts into the space. He walks up to each audience member's car, peering inside and laughing. He strides to the covered cars and dramatically pulls off the sheet, revealing Boy 1 and Girl in the driving seats of two boy racer cars. They rev their engines.

GIRL. It all starts with a ...

BOY 1. It all ends with a ...

GIRL. Not with a whimper.

BOY 1. No fear. No fear.

BOY 2. What are you expecting?

GIRL. When you've gotta go.

BOY 1. You've gotta go.

ALL. Go!

The two cars speed off in opposite directions.

GIRL. Keep her lit.

BOY 1. One hundred and ten!

BOY 2. He clocks it up Larch Hill.

GIRL. Speed of light.

BOY 1. Fishtailing at one twenty.

BOY 2. *[Whispers]* Keep her lit!

GIRL. And we haven't an axe to grind.

GIRL+BOY 2. We just ...

BOY 2. He's losing his grip.

Boy 1 drives back into the space, skidding to a halt beside the third parked car.

GIRL+BOY 2. We're just having...

BOY 2. He's drifting. He's drifting.

GIRL+BOY 2. We're just...

GIRL. Just like everyone else.

BOY 2. Then...

A siren blares. Boy 1 is thrown back and appears to be weightlessly floating inside the car. A new soundscape surges to the fore. We hear the sound of astronauts doing a space walk as Boy 1 floats about inside the car.

BOY 2. Cracks open. Skulls back the champagne.

GIRL. She goes like a rocket boss, like a rocket into space.

BOY 2. Weightless bodies. No reverse.

GIRL. Yeah, that's right Einstein. No reverse on this beast of a thing.

BOY 2. Speed of light.

BOY 1. Dark.

GIRL. Black.

BOY 2. Stop.

The interior of the car goes black. We hear funeral bells. Boy 2 stands with head bowed beside the parked car. Boy 1 gets out of the car and stands beside him.

BOY 1. Big turn out. Massive.

BOY 2. And today as we celebrate the life of this young man ...

BOY 1. So young.

BOY 2. Everyone who knew him will tell you he was a young man who ...

BOY 1. A waste, such a waste.

BOY 2. And the question, the painful question that we, as a society, must ask each time we face such a terrible tragedy is ...

BOY 1. *[To audience]* What are you looking at?

The dark dissonant soundtrack comes to the fore.

BOY 2. *[Whispers]* Keep her lit.

BOY 1. Nobody's dead.

BOY 2. No fear. Not yet.

BOY 1. We're just ...

BOY 2. We're just having ...

BOY 1. We're just ...

BOY 2. We're ... forget it.

BOY 1. They wouldn't ...

BOY 2. Just wouldn't ...

BOY 1. Nah.

Low throbbing trance music gives the idea of anticipation. Boy 1 and Boy 2 parade across the space admiring their cars and squaring up to each other.

BOY 2. She's got a 1.5 litre six cylinder turbo.

BOY 1. She's a 1.2 litre rotary – They call it a Wankel engine.

BOY 2. Got 175 break horse power.

Boy 1 and Boy 2 open the bonnets of two audience member's cars.

BOY 1. Rotary. No pistons. She keeps on spooling.

BOY 2. Six cylinder twin cam.

BOY 1. Rotary. She uses gravity. That's what NASA used in their rockets and stuff.

BOY 2. Rear wheel drive.

Boy 1 and Boy 2 close the bonnets simultaneously.

BOY 1. Completely stripped her out. Put in the set of roll bars.

BOY 2. 180 break standard which isn't bad for a 1.2.

BOY 1. Nought to sixty in about 4.8 seconds. About that. Yeah.

BOY 2. This is a twin turbo version. Not the single turbo version.

BOY 1. But I mean she's got a bigger front-mounted intercooler. Put that in myself.

BOY 2. When I change the brain of the car it'll probably give me an extra 150 break horse power – straight out.

BOY 1. All the same. I'd say she's a lovely safe car.

BOY 2. Sticks to the tarmac like ... tar.

BOY 1. Tar.

Boy 2 and Boy 1 take out a picnic rug and flask. They arrange it carefully on the bonnet of a car and pour tea accompanied by a twee Mozart theme. Boy 2 and Boy 1 adopt a middle-aged genteel persona.

BOY 1. Well I don't drive fast myself.

BOY 2. I've never actually been in a crash.

BOY 1. I'm very careful on the road.

BOY 2. Well maybe just one time.

BOY 1. But everyone has the odd crash.

BOY 2. I didn't really stick around ... at the scene.

BOY 1. In fairness, there were no real fatalities.

BOY 2. Hit and run. I mean what does that actually mean? I drove away. And the state of my paintwork. That cost me a few ton.

BOY 1. But anyway. I don't drive fast. Not as fast as I used to. No.

BOY 2. No.

BOY 1. Yeah, the rotary.

BOY 2. Very safe on the roads.

BOY 1. That's what NASA use in their rockets ... *[Threatening]* and stuff!

Boy 1 and Boy 2 put away the picnic things in one of the performance cars. Boy 2 leaves the space.

Now, Boy 1 adopts a new persona. He prowls around his souped-up car, caressing its curves – worshipping his motor. The slow-build music of Rockets Fall on Rocket Falls by Godspeed You! Black Emperor plays. Boy 1 jumps into his car through the window. Girl walks slowly and purposefully into the central space, illuminated by a spotlight. She pauses to throw balletic poses as she approaches the car. Boy 1 is transfixed. Girl stops in front of the car, holding Boy 1's gaze.

GIRL. I don't see Derek. I see …

BOY 1. 1.4 litre, 8 valve.

GIRL. I see …

BOY 1. 250 break horse power.

GIRL. I see a …

BOY 1. Spoilers. Vents. Go Faster.

GIRL. I see a getaway car.

BOY 1. Booting it.

GIRL. Backroads, boreens, red lights.

BOY 1. The fast. The furious.

GIRL. Past prams, pedestrians.

BOY 1. Burning rubber.

GIRL. Leaving those losers behind.

BOY 1. Not like us.

Girl gets into the car and slams the door shut.

GIRL. In our getaway car.

Boy 1 drives the car in a circle around the parked car.

BOY 1. Not like us in our …

GIRL. Step on it!

BOY 1. To the metal.

GIRL. Faster!

BOY 1. Floorin' it. Floorin' it.

GIRL. Faster! I need to get away from all of this.

BOY 1. Away from?

GIRL. Please.

BOY 1. Away from?

GIRL. I can't take it.

BOY 1. What's wrong?

GIRL. My father ... he ... he...

BOY 1. What?

GIRL. Since I was little ... He...

BOY 1. No!

GIRL. He ... I can't take it ...

Boy 1 skids to a halt.

BOY 1. I'm going to fucking kill him.

GIRL. He drives an Opel fucking Corsa! And I'm so bored!!

BOY 1. What?

GIRL. There's nothing to do, nothing for the young people, and boo hoo hoo. All that stuff so just step on it!

BOY 1. What?

A dramatic news 'sting'. Girl pops out of the car window sitting on the sill and using the top of the car as a kind of news desk. She adopts an intellectual/TV presenter persona.

GIRL. In an affluent society with a massive increase in average disposable income, many young people are spending their money on vehicles, cars, motors. This can lead to greater mobility for the individual but also to the individualisation of society as a whole.

BOY 1. What?

GIRL. Is it any wonder? The 'Me Culture', everyone in their own metal box, unwilling to accept their duties to, and impact on, the wider structure of society.

BOY 1. What?

GIRL. An out-of-control car-slash-consumerist culture where 'success has four wheels'.

BOY 1. What?

GIRL. Just step on it! Drive! Go!

ZZ Top's Sharp Dressed Man *plays. The car drives off at top speed, burning rubber.*

Cool Water *by Spiritualized plays. Boy 2 wanders into the centre of the space swigging a can of cheap lager. He looks up and down the road. A recorded monologue (below) emerges over the music. Boy 1 speeds up in open-top sports car – rolls up, horn blaring. Girl is already in the car. Boy 2 jumps in. The car moves off, but this time very slowly. The actors move in slow-motion now. The car moves in circles around the space in front of the audience's cars. The actors drink, scream, punch the air and shout abuse at the audience. They hurl water bombs at their cars.*

I don't expect you to support the Bhoys, hang furry dice in your car, listen to techno.

I don't expect you to wear a tracksuit.

I don't expect you to drive through my estate.

I don't expect you to fancy my girlfriend.

I don't expect you to enjoy my tyres squealing past midnight.

I don't expect you to know what it's like to put the foot down.

I don't expect you to race me up the back roads.

I don't expect you to clock it round blind corners, rubber smoking.

I don't expect you to get pissed, get high and drive.

Suddenly, everything jolts back into real time. The car drives off at top speed.

I don't expect you to remember what it's like to be young.

I don't expect you to understand.

The car turns and parks outside the central space. Girl and Boy 2 walk slowly back towards centre of the yard. Boy 1 stands beside his car watching them.

I don't expect you to think anything else except scum, boy racer scum.

Girl and Boy 2 embrace.

Until I'm dead.

I don't expect you to come to my funeral.

But you'll all be there.

To pay your respects.

A jazzy shuffle beat plays. The boy and girl break from their embrace and begin to dance together.

BOY 2. You look up to me.

GIRL. Not as much as the Duffer.

BOY 2. You look up to me. I'm young.

GIRL. Listen.

BOY 2. Do you want to die?

GIRL. Has he got your attention?

BOY 2. Old people are excellent drivers.

GIRL. Fact.

BOY 2. Even over the limit.

GIRL. Fact.

BOY 2. Young people are not.

GIRL. And another thing.

BOY 2. Would you ever slow down?

GIRL. There's young lunatics racing up that road every night of the week.

BOY 2. Mam never broke the speed limit.

GIRL. Aghh! Late for the school play.

BOY 2. Beeep!

GIRL. Stupid fucking lorry!

BOY 2. But we're not here to talk about that.

GIRL. We're here to talk about you.

BOY 2. The youth.

GIRL. Where do you get off?

BOY 2. Where did you get this obsession with cars?

GIRL. Clogging up the roads.

BOY 2. Total gridlock.

GIRL. Yield right of way.

BOY 2. The auld man's late for work.

GIRL. Seen his new car? Nippy. Very nippy.

BOY 2. Which brings me on to the government.

GIRL. The Minister was in a hurry.

BOY 2. Missed the flight from Kerry.

GIRL. Hopped in the Merc.

BOY 2. That man is a guard.

GIRL. Vroom.

BOY 2 He's a highly trained driver.

GIRL. Vroom. Vroom

BOY 2. It's not a crime.

GIRL. To go 50.

BOY 2. Or 60.

GIRL. Over the limit.

BOY 2. He's a guard.

GIRL. Minister's got an appointment.

BOY 2. Gay is waiting.

GIRL. The big launch.

BOY 2. Gay's an excellent driver.

GIRL. Road Safety 101.

BOY 2. An integrated governmental response to the scourge of young drivers.

GIRL. Guard. Put the foot down.

BOY 2. Excellent driver.

GIRL. Gay is waiting.

The dance ends. A slow sexy funk track plays. Boy 2 picks up a newspaper and reads aloud.

BOY 2. He was obviously going into shock. He was continuously pacing, trying to get back into the field where the car was and his breathing was very fast, she said. He asked me if they (his passengers) were okay.

Boy 1 drives into the yard. Girl thumbs a lift with Boy 1. They drive towards Boy 2 stopping just in front of him.

I didn't tell him they were dead. The woman was giving evidence at the trial of Kurtis Dolan (twenty-one) who denies four counts of death by dangerous driving and ...

Boy 2 passes the newspaper to Girl.

GIRL. The accident happened on the main Galway to Dublin road on July 23 after the accused overtook another car and lost control, crashing into the car carrying James and Stephanie Dunne and their 15-year old-daughter, Christine ... car was travelling at up to 100 miles per hour and the force of the impact sent his car into a 360-degree spin in the centre of the road ... no memory of the accident.

Boy 1 takes the paper and gets out of the car. He walks slowly out of the yard and up the road. Girl gets out of the car and goes to Boy 2. They and kiss and then run together to the parked car. Inside the car they undress each other and embrace passionately.

BOY 1. Lost their lives when the Nissan Micra in which they were travelling went out of control and hit a lamppost ... a local woman said: I could see there had been a crash. There were two people lying on the grass in front of the car. I thought for a minute they must have gotten out through the back door. But then they started to take the bodies away. They were dead, so they had obviously been thrown from the car somehow.

BOY 2. Lost control of the car and crashed through fencing and trees and then into the lamppost. An ambulance spokesman said: 'We could not get him out. We were trying to resuscitate him while he was in the car, but it was very difficult. We did our best to keep him alive.

Boy 1 drives at high speed through the yard. We hear the sound of a massive crash. The space goes dark. The 'Queen of the Night' aria from Mozart's Magic Flute *plays. A red spotlight illuminates the parked car. Girl falls out of the car door and stumbles away from the car. She is wearing red. She staggers like some drunken bedraggled diva wandering into the spotlight before her cue. Confused. Hair tangled. She cries out for help but her call is drowned by the music. She clambers onto the bonnet of the car and collapses. The aria is killed in mid flow by an ugly thud. The space goes dark apart from the glow of a light inside the open top car. A long silence. Then we hear real interview footage of fathers whose children died in a road accidents.*

FATHER 1. One of his friends got killed in an accident, two of his friends in fact. And he came home for that and he didn't go back. And that accident was roughly a year before the one that he was in. And the thing about it is, there's six of them buried together, all friends, in the one piece of a graveyard in Cockhill, and they were all killed in road accidents.

FATHER 2. Well, she was full of life. Never sat down a whole lot. Always on the move. Bubbly. Full of life, you know. She was doing hairdressing in the tech in Derry and she had a wee part time job in the town, three days a week. And that's what she was doing. She'd have been qualified now, if she'd lived till now. She'd have been fully qualified.

FATHER 1. I'm afraid just every night. And I wake up at nights with nightmares. This is going on a long time now. Thinking I see flashers. And I even look out the windows but it's all flashbacks from the accident.

FATHER 2. The house is dead quiet at night. She always had someone in, friends up in the room, dressing up to go out and things like that. None of that now. We miss all that.

FATHER 1. There's not one morning that I get up, that I don't think about him. There's not one night that I don't think about him. When I'm putting the dinners out, I'm always thinking of him, I'm always thinking that he's there. And when I'm putting the dinners out, I think there's something wrong. I haven't enough. And then I cop on that he's not there.

In the darkness we see the silhouette of Boy 1. He slowly walks to the open-top car parked in the middle of the space and turns off the light. All three actors slowly and silently walk away into the darkness of the night.

LIZZIE LAVELLE AND THE VANISHING OF EMLYCLOUGH

Author's Note

Lizzie Lavelle and the Vanishing of Emlyclough is a site-specific piece, commissioned by Mayo County Council (Ireland). It was created for performance in a natural amphitheatre in the sand dunes just off the 15th fairway at Carne Golf Links, Belmullet, County Mayo. The play was inspired by the history, folklore, landscape and people of the Mullet Peninsula – one of the West of Ireland's Gaeltacht (Irish-speaking) regions. The text is bilingual (Irish-English) with **all Irish dialogue in bold** followed by an English translation in brackets.

Lizzie Lavelle and the Vanishing of Emlyclough was premiered at Carne Golf Links, Belmullet, County Mayo in July 2007. The play was produced by The Performance Corporation.

Original Cast

Paul Connaughton
Niamh Daly
Eamon Hunt
Cillian O'Donnachadha
Lisa Lambe
Noni Stapleton
Stephen Swift
Members of Phoenix Players, Belmullet

Director: Jo Mangan
Set Designer: Sinead O'Hanlon
Costume Designers: Sinead Cuthbert & Therese McKeone
Irish Dialogue Translator: Fiona Ní Dhuibhir
Composer: Sam Jackson

SCENE 1

The audience walks from the clubhouse of Carne golf course into the sand dunes. Along the path there are transistor radios blaring out a frantic match commentary. There's an atmosphere of a big match day. Soon the audience have left the golf course behind and are in the wild dunes. They find themselves in a giant hollow in the sand. To left and right are two 30 metre peaks, and out ahead of them lies the Atlantic. Then, in the side of the dune something shifts. A hand emerges, then a foot, then the body of Sandman struggles free from the sand-face. The old man realizes that he is not alone.

SANDMAN. You're gone a bit off the fairway, aren't ye? Ye may forget about your golf ball.

Sandman nods towards his sandy bed.

Bhí aithne agam ar fear tráth (I knew a man once) Once upon a time. He was an Emlyclough man. Doesn't matter if he was north or if he was south. The thing is, he was out harvesting snails, **mar a bhí sé de nós acu a dhéanamh ag an am** (as used to be the way with them). And wasn't he hauling a hundredweight sack of them tasty molluscs up this very sandy bank. **Nuair a shocraigh sé suí síos ar feadh noiméad, a anál a tharraingt agus sult a bhaint as toit. Ar an spota seo go díreach a bhí sé ach ...** (And this man, didn't he take the notion to sit down for a sup of smoke right here on this very spot). All they found of that man was his pipe. Hadn't he fallen sound asleep, and woken up seven feet under. I'm warning you. Sand has a terrible habit. In time, it covers everything – buries the good and the bad without explanation. Then marram grass and green moss creep in to complete the work. **Ní chreideann sibh mé?** (You don't believe me?) Sure didn't it do for them two quarrelsome parishes of Emlyclough North and Emlyclough South. **Anois sin scéal agaibh.** (Now there's a story for you). Aren't they buried right here. Under your back-stick. I'll tell you, they were too mithered with faction fighting to notice the sand was starting to come up around their oxters. Sure the wherefore and the why of that fight are lost in the sand among a million other grains of truth. **Ach déaraidh mé é seo libh** – (But I'm telling you this) It was on the Ball pitch that they played out that furious disliking.

SCENE 2

Over the crest of the giant dune, a giant ball tumbles and nestles in the bottom of the hollow. Silence. Then a blood-curdling war cry. The Ball teams of North and South Emlyclough come helter-skelter over the top of the dunes and into the hollow. The Ball is won by south, then wrestled away by north. It's a hell for leather contest but no one seems to know what the objective is. The action is pursued by a manic commentator.

COMMENTATOR. A dhaoine uaisle (Ladies and gentlemen) you have us discovered in the dying minutes of this all-Erris Ball final and what a mighty reckoning it's turned out to be! In shades of red, the legendary Emlyclough South and in hues of green, the mighty Emlyclough North. **D'fhéadfá a rá gur beirt fhoireann iad seo atá an dearg ghráin acu ar a chéile!** (And it's surely fair to say there is no love lost between these two teams)**.** On day one of this match we had the unfortunate off-the-Ball drowning of North full forward Dinny John Padden at Danish Cellar. And on day three South full back Larry Lavelle had more than one leg amputated as he soared high to collect the Ball back at Annagh Head. Surely, ladies and gentlemen, this is the very stuff. Surely, this is what the game of Ball is all about. **'Sé ár n-oidhreacht é, ár ndúchas, ár tradisiún. (**It's part of what we are, it's our way of life, it's our tradition). It's about passion, about pride, about raw bloodthirsty hate. And there's no finer example of that voluptuous spirit than here among the sandy-banks of Emlyclough. Here we have two proud parishes who – not to put too fine a point on it – despise each others guts! **Seachtain ó shoin a thosaigh an cluiche ollmhór seo** (One week ago this mighty match began). And it's been a week that's seen that ball booted, hacked and tackled up, down and around every squared inch of the Mullet peninsula. And now, finally, conclusively, after seven days of such great excitement, we find ourselves in injury time – and of that there has been plenty – with the score standing at **Ceithre chúl, dhá chéad ochtú naoi cúilín go Emlyclough Thuaidh. Agus dhá chúl, dhá chéad naocha cúig cúilín go Emlyclough Theas** (4 goals and 289 points to Emlyclough North, and 2 goals and 295 to Emlyclough South). Yes, ladies and gentlemen it's level pegging! Level pegging as they slog it out right on the border of these two mighty parishes. Who can rupture this murdering deadlock?

MICHAEL. *[to audience]* **An bhfuil laoch ar an bpáirc seo inniú?** (Who will be the hero of the hour?) Could it be that Ball wizard at full forward, that hero of Emlyclough North, young

Michael Meenaghan? **B'fhéidir gur'b é seo a sheans mór** (This might be his big chance). The Ball flies high in the air just outside the South goalmouth.

LIZZIE. *[to audience]* **Ach fan. Cé seo ag teacht inár dtreo?** (But wait, who have we here?) It's the darling of Emlyclough South, the legendary Lizzie Lavelle. Perhaps the most talent-laden player of her generation, and certainly the most attractive, this should present no difficulty.

As Lizzie goes for the Ball she is struck by a thunderbolt. She spots Michael for the first time. It's love at first sight.

COMMENTATOR. Ó, a Mhaighdean! Tá sé caillte aici. Tá an liathróid caillte ag Lizzie Lavelle. (But no! She's dropped it. She's dropped the Ball). And surely a chance here for Michael Meenaghan – his father a snail farmer, his mother a marram grass weaver-woman, just like their parents before them, staunch people of Emlyclough North.

Michael collects the Ball with ease, but then he too is struck by the thunderbolt – caught in the laser beam of Lizzie's stare. He too falls instantly in love. The stare between the two lingers. The Ball drops from Michael's arms.

But no! Seconds to go and Meenaghan's been hacked down in the area by Lavelle's shimmering smile. **Bhuel ní luíonn sé sin le spiorad an spórt bhreá seo go deimhin!** (Well that's certainly not in the spirit of this fine sport!)

The two teams roar blue murder at each of their players urging them to get the Ball.

He's only got eyes for Lizzie and vice versa! Just moments ago those deadly adversaries North and South were locked in bloody battle but now it would seem they're about to be locked in a ...

Lizzie and Michael move towards each other, filled with desire. The full time whistle blows.

A draw! It's a draw! **Beidh lá eile ag Emlyclough Thuaidh agus Emlyclough Theas, a cháirde Gael.** (Emlyclough North and Emlyclough South will have to do it all over again. Ladies and gents), It's a replay!

The North team surrounds Lizzie, shouting abuse at her for putting their player off in such an underhand manner while the South team surround Michael, infuriated by his romantic approaches to Lizzie. There's a melee in the middle of the field as the sides square up to each other, but in the chaos Lizzie and Michael reach out for each other. Their fingers touch for a moment, then they're pulled apart.

MICHAEL. Cad is ainm duit?! (What is your name?!)

LIZZIE. I'm Lizzie, Lizzie Lavelle! **Cad is ainm duit'se?** (What's yours?)

MICHAEL. Michael, Michael Meenaghan is the name me mother gave me!

The rabbles of north and south storm off noisily in either direction carrying Lizzie and Michael with them. A calm descends. The only people left are Lizzie's Father and Michael's Mother.

MOTHER. I have seen you Southies turn many a mucky trick in my time, but I never witnessed filthier than that. That Lizzie of yours is some class of a vixen mesmerizing my Michael with her flattering eyelashes!

FATHER. Seafóid! (Rubbish!) The girls of Emlyclough South are purer than driven sand and Lizzie's the purest of them all.

Mother folds her arms with a disbelieving snort.

'Sé'n Michael sin agat'sa is cúis leis. (That Michael of yours had cause in it.) Not to mind yourself missus, for raring a gigolo stud of a son!

MOTHER. Nach íontach an tuairim atá agat díot féin. (Don't flatter your own self.) My son wouldn't want no grass with that girl – no mind what pervert notions she might have entered into her head.

FATHER. Níl ach nóisean amháin ina ceann aici. (Just one notion she'll enter.) To hack seven shades of sand out of your own son when the replay comes about. Until then I won't permit Lizzie Lavelle getting next nor near your Michael.

MOTHER. Good!

FATHER. Good!

MOTHER. Good.

FATHER. Good.

In full agreement for once in their lives, they don't know what to do.

MOTHER. Right.

FATHER. Right.

MOTHER. I'll spy you at the replay.

FATHER. Not if I spy you first.

Mother and Father go their separate ways.

SCENE 3

From the crest of the dune there's a shrill whistle, and another. Over the brow of the hill creeps Michael, furtively looking back. Over the brow of the hill opposite marches Lizzie, full of defiance. Michael doesn't see her and gives another whistle.

LIZZIE. Thall anseo! Anseo atá mé a phleota! (About here! I'm here you daft latchako!)

MICHAEL. Shhhh, cloisfidh siad muid. (Shush, they'll hear.) There'll be a holy blue murder if a person spies us.

LIZZIE. No person's going to stop me being with my man.

She grabs Michael and kisses him passionately, he goes weak at the knees.

MICHAEL. OK.

A moment of sweetness.

LIZZIE. So Michael Meenaghan. You're not above at training with the mighty men of Emlyclough North. You must have good reasoning for it. The replay is in two weeks.

MICHAEL. Hokey I know, I know. **Marófar mé.** (I'll be killed.)

A raised eyebrow from Lizzie.

But that's OK because I'm with my beautiful darling Lizzie Lavelle.

LIZZIE. So you're going to line out for them?

MICHAEL. I've been informed if I don't line out I'll be beaten, tied and dumped on the dune for the sand to swallow me live. *[beat]* Mammy means the best but she's a hard woman to contradict.

LIZZIE. Bhuel, ní bheidh mise ag imirt. (Well, I'm not playing.)

MICHAEL. Jesus Lizzie they haven't dropped you?

LIZZIE. Roghnaíodh mé, alright. (I've been picked alright.) But I've had my fill. Sure, isn't it all a collection of miserable nonsense. Spy me father. Ever since mam was killed in the big game last year he's mad as a pebble with the obsession of besting your lot. **Ní rachaidh mise an bóthar céanna leis. No way.** (I won't finish up like him. I won't.) So, I'm going to tell them enough is plenty. I'm not playing. Anyway, a person doesn't want to be marking her sweetheart. A crunching tackle is a terrible thing Michael.

Lizzie gives a flirtatious glance towards Michael's groin. Michael winces slightly.

MICHAEL. But Lizzie, he'll take a murder on you.

LIZZIE. What about him?

MICHAEL. Ó, a Dhia, Lizzie. Tar liom as an áit seo. (Oh God Lizzie, please. Come away with me.) We can take off to somewhere far – to a big city where no one cares who we are or where we come from.

LIZZIE. I told you, I'm not moving to Belmullet. They'll just have to accept us here in Emlyclough. **Seo ár mbaile (**This is our own home.)

MICHAEL. Ó, Lizzie ... tá mé i ngrá leat. (Oh Lizzie. I love you.)

A rash impulse overtakes Michael.

Wed me. Wed me Lizzie Lavelle of the parish of Emlyclough south.

LIZZIE. Yes! Yes, I will wed you Michael Meenaghan of the parish of Emlyclough north.

They kiss.

MICHAEL. Tá an ceart agat. (You're right.) Damn the rest of them all to Bangor! **Fanfaidh mise 'gus tusa anseo. (**We'll stay put.) We'll buy a farm of land – half on the south, half on the north. The sand here is deep and fertile. I'll harvest the snails and you'll weave the marram grass. And between us we'll be happy as larks. And if a person, any person tries putting a stop to us, I'll fight them. And I'll never ever stop fighting for you, and for our life together if that's the necessary.

LIZZIE. Oh Michael, is it a promise?

MICHAEL. It's a promise.

Father and Mother charge into the hollow from opposite sides.

FATHER. Promise me back stick! Get a distance away from my daughter.

MOTHER. Take your hands off that southern yoke! **Ní imreóidh mac ar bith liom'sa le duine ón bhfoireann eile.** (No son of mine plays with the other team.)

Father grabs Lizzie and drags her away screaming. Furious, Michael tries to save her. But Mother's thugs hold Michael back and he too is dragged back to his home place.

SCENE 4

In ambles Sandman.

SANDMAN. Anois, an bhfeiceann sibh céard atá i gceist agam? (Do you see now what I mean?) A furious disliking. And so those two unlikely lovers are separated like two grains of sand – one thrown hither and the other thrown the opposite direction. Every single night, by the scruff of her craw, Lizzie Lavelle is dragged to training and likewise for Michael Meenaghan. Every single night the teams gallop up Tower Hill and back down ten times and finish with a sprint to Blacksod Point. Light training just. But what hurts that lovey-dovey pair a consideration more than training is the heart-yanking separation. **Mar níl Lizzie in ann a hintinn a dhíriú ar thada ach Michael. Agus is amhlaidh dhó.** (For Lizzie can think of nothing but Michael and he the same for her.)

The lovers appear up on the ridge at opposite sides of the hollow. They shout to each other but can't hear each other. They wave semaphore flags but still the confusion is evident and their lack of communication is leading to frustration.

But a time comes when it feels like their love is just another fist-full of sand, slipping away grain by grain.

LIZZIE. You said you'd fight for me Michael Meenaghan!

SANDMAN. *[to audience]* Long distance relationships ...

MICHAEL. Céard é?! (What?!)

SANDMAN. *[sighs]* Never easy.

LIZZIE. Cén fáth nach ndéanann tú tárthál orm?! (Why won't you rescue me?!)

MICHAEL. What?!

LIZZIE. You said you'd fight for me! You don't love me!

MICHAEL. Go luath. Tiocfaidh mé go luath. (Soon. I'll come soon.)

LIZZIE. What?!

MICHAEL. Mo ghrá thú, Lizzie! (I love you Lizzie!)

LIZZIE. Then prove it Michael! Fight for me like your promise!

MICHAEL. Soon!

LIZZIE. Tá mo chroí briste gan thú, Michael! (My heart is dying without you Michael!) You've got to come and get me right now!

MICHAEL. Foighid ort, Lizzie, más é so thoil é! Foighid ort! (Please Lizzie! Be patient!)

LIZZIE. Patient!? Daddy's right! Emlyclough North men are nothing but lazy, lying, dirty snails!

Lizzie dissolves in tears, and runs off.

SCENE 5

Michael is left alone. Mother appears from nowhere, as mothers often do.

MOTHER. Mo mhacín bán. Mo stór, mo leanbh. My son. My only own darling son. You have made your mother very proud. You showed her. You gave that awful ... yoke her marching orders.

MICHAEL. Mam, you've the wrong end of the ...

MOTHER. Decent North men like my own son don't wash their socks in a dirty stream.

MICHAEL. Ah, Mam. A person can't say the like of ...

MOTHER. Because you know that bits the like of them South women are nothing but a bunch of ... Floozies!

MICHAEL. Mam. No.

MOTHER. Nothing but a ... *[tourette's spasm]* Vixens!

MICHAEL. Stop, a Mhamaí! (Mammy. Stop it.)

MOTHER. Everyone knows they'll ditch their ... *[tourette's spasm]* Heifers! ... at the drop of a ... Trollops!

MICHAEL. Imigh leat abhaile, a mham. (Mam, go away home.)

MOTHER. A mhac? (Son?)

MICHAEL. Away home and wash your mouth out.

MOTHER. A mhac?! (Son!)

MICHAEL. I won't hear you talk as such about the girl I love.

MOTHER. A mhac? (Son?)

Mother tries to check his temperature but Michael's having none of it.

MICHAEL. Lizzie Lavelle is the girl I intend to marry!

MOTHER. Oh dear Hokie in heaven. She's put you under some sort of ... Strumpet! You've fallen under her ... Minx! Hussy! Jezebel!

Michael grabs hold of Mother and shakes her until she breaks out of her fit.

MICHAEL. All this roaring and ranting has me sick in the gut. This absurdity of hatred has you pinched. Now please mother. Go home.

Mother runs off wailing and keening about how a strumpet of the south has snared her son.

SCENE 6

Michael turns from his departing mother and faces the steep slope of the sand cliff.

SANDMAN. Don chéad uair riamh ina shaol, (For the first time in his life,) Michael Meenaghan makes his own mind up, on his own. He isn't going to let that fist-full of precious sand slip-slide out between his own fingers. He's going to fight for that girl like he promised. **Agus mar sin, déanann sé a bhealach tríd an ghleanna agus dreapann sé an sliabh.** (And so he treks through the valley and he climbs that mountain.)

Michael begins to climb the cliff. Half way up he looks down at the dizzying drop to certain death but he continues to climb despite his fear.

He is going to get the rescuing of that girl, they're going to be together. And isn't that the solitary thing that keeps him going as he climbs the insurmountable cliff of Emlyclough south.

He makes it to the top of the cliff. But along the ridge pop up the fearsome men of Emlyclough South, just like Red Indians about to strike. The Emlyclough men are agile. They close in on Michael. The boy fights the good fight. Many of the Emlyclough men are hurled from that high place. But finally Michael is overcome by Lizzie's angry father.

FATHER. Off with you and your lechery! Off and buzz about your own kind. **Go dtiocfaidh thiar aniar ní leagfaidh tú lámh ar m'iníon'se.** (You'll never have my own daughter.)

MICHAEL. But why? I love her. I'll be good to her.

FATHER. You know the why.

MICHAEL. But I don't. Tell me. **Cén sórt ciall a bhaineann le stop a chuir leis an ngrá atá ag duine ón Tuaisceart do dhuine ón bhfoireann eile?** (Can't see the why or the wherefore stopping a person from loving a person who plays for the other team.)

FATHER. Lark talk and backchat!

MICHAEL. But can anyone remember what this way of feuding and fighting and hating is all about?

FATHER. Sin mar a tháinig sé anuas chugainn. (It's tradition.) There's bad sand between us. That's the way we like it.

MICHAEL. But I love Lizzie.

FATHER. Ní leat'sa í le grá a thabhairt di. (She's not yours to love.) Now hump off!

With that, down the slope he's tumbled by Father.

SCENE 7

Michael is a defeated man. He picks up a suitcase and takes a last look around his home-place.

SANDMAN. Michael bocht. (Poor Michael.) So near and yet so far. It's a shame Lizzie will never know how hard he fought to save her. **Agus mar sin – croíbhriste agus náirithe, tosaíonn Michael Meenaghan ar a chuid málaí a phacáil.** (And so, brimming with hurt and shame Michael Meenaghan packs his bags.) It's the night before the replay of the All-Erris final and he has his sights set across the water on the city of Cricklehead. Maybe there he can forget Lizzie Lavelle, **an cailín ó Emlyclough Theas.** (the girl from Emlyclough South.)

He picks up a photo of Lizzie, caressing the frame, then carefully places it in the case. He slowly walks out of the hollow towards the Atlantic Ocean, suitcase in hand.

But sure isn't true love like sand? It gets everywhere. And just when you think you have it all shook off, a few grains are hiding within in some cranny – itching and itching.

SCENE 8

SANDMAN. But Michael wasn't the only one who escaped from sandy-banks of Emlyclough that night.

Lizzie enters pursued by Granger, a sleazy older man in tight swimming trunks. He's laughing. She's trying to carry an array of beach equipment including buckets, spades, a lilo etc. Lizzie is in a state of dismay.

LIZZIE. I said no!

GRANGER. What? Don't you like the Lamptons? Don't you like having fun. That's what we're here for.

LIZZIE. I'm here to do work.

GRANGER. Come on. I was only kidding with you. It didn't mean nothing. What's the problem? You've got a boyfriend?

LIZZIE. No.

GRANGER. OK. I get it. Come over here and sit down. Let's talk about it. He's probably no good anyhow. Come over. Sit down. OK. Let's talk about the movies. I'm a very powerful person. You're a very pretty girl. Let's see what we can do, all right?

Lizzie shakes her head.

What? You don't want to be in the movies. Come here.

Lizzie shakes her head again.

I said come here! You little ...

Granger makes a lunge for Lizzie. This time there's no playing. Lizzie screams and runs away pursued by Granger. Yolanda, a matronly Cuban maid, comes bustling and witnesses the scene.

YOLANDA. Ee-Ho day poota. Al-ways thee same. Escuse me! Escuse me sir! Sir! I make joo a nice Heen-Tonn-eeka?

GRANGER. Scram! I'm auditioning.

Granger catches Lizzie and wrestles her to the ground. She is not enjoying the audition.

YOLANDA. Joor Heen-Tonn-eeka ees ready for joo.

GRANGER. Yolanda. Go Away!

Yolanda bends down to speak to Granger who's on the ground with Lizzie struggling underneath.

YOLANDA. Sir? Sir? Ay make it like joo like it sirr – with a troth-EEto of lee-MON an mucho ice.

GRANGER. I don't want it!

Yolanda throws the gin and tonic in Granger's face, instantly cooling his frenzy.

YOLANDA. Ay. Ay trip.

Wiping his face dry, Granger releases Lizzie who scuttles for cover at Yolanda's apron strings.

All I joos wan-ed to say joo was joor wife she's comin – with the kiddies. I can make joo O-tra Heen-Tonn-eeka eef joo arr steel a liddle thurs-tee.

Granger storms off. Lizzie cries.

YOLANDA. Ay! Dios mee-o neenya. Joo arr farr from home.

Lizzie nods.

An in love.

Lizzie throws a surprised glance.

Ay. Yolanda know what ees like to be farr away from the man joo love. Venga. Tell Yolanda ev-erry-tin. Ees he handsome?

LIZZIE. He is that. And he's strong and kind and everything you'd want in a ... He swore he'd fight for me. He swore he'd rescue me. He swore he loved me but ...

Yolanda cradles poor Lizzie in her arms and sings the Cuban love song 'No me vayas a engañar'. They depart the scene singing together.

SCENE 9

Mack and AJ, a pair of tough Dublin builders, enter. They do the least amount of work possible. One 'supervises' while the other makes halfhearted efforts at work. Michael enters in a bit of a fluster.

MICHAEL. God lads, you're going to kill me.

MACK. Ah don't tell me!

MICHAEL. I went the up and down of Cricklehead High Street and I swear to you, nowhere could I find them rubber nails.

MACK. Ah sufferin' Jaysus!

AJ. Never mind the rubber nails. What about the other thing?

Michael shakes his head.

What did I tell you? What did I tell you?!

MICHAEL. Don't show your face back here without the glass hammer.

Mack and AJ burst out laughing.

AJ. Glass Hammer!

MACK. Rubber Nails!

The gaffer enters in a rage.

GAFFER. Oi! Get to work! I said get to work! Don't you understand English?

MACK. Tá an t-amadán anseo. (The eejit's here)

AJ. *[to Gaffer]* **Ní thuigeann muid.** (We don't understand.)

MACK. Ceard a duirt sé?

GAFFER. I got the real dregs here, ain't I. You're here to work. Work. Understand?

The men pretend they misunderstand and proceed to sit down and take a break.

You're joking. You're joking me now. Get up! Come on off your arse and do some work.

The Gaffer grabs a shovel from one of the men and starts to work to demonstrate.

MACK. Ar ndóigh, beidh an jab ar fad déanta aige má leanann sé air. (He'll have the job done in its whole entirety if he keeps going like that.)

MICHAEL. *[in English]* He will. He'll have it all done for us if he keeps going.

GAFFER. *[furious]* Think you can take the mickey out of me? Think you're clever. Well you're not. Dragged yourself out of the quicksand so you think you're something special. I've seen hundreds of sandy little scumbags like you in my time. I destroyed 'em all. See that lot? *[points at dune]* You get all that shifted, gone, every grain of sand, by tonight.

WORKERS. Yes sir, yes sir, yes sir ...

GAFFER. Otherwise you're out on your ear. Yeah, you understand now, don't you!

WORKERS. Yes sir, yes sir, yes sir ...

The men make a start at the work but the minute the gaffer is gone Mack and AJ stop working. But Michael keeps going, working energetically. Mack and AJ lean on their shovels, smirking.

MICHAEL. Come on lads? You don't expect me to do it all on me own, do you?

MACK. All that hard work'll set you in grand gigolo shape for your girlfriend.

MICHAEL. I don't have a girlfriend.

AJ. That's not what I heard. I heard you'd need to be fit for that lassie of yours. I heard Lizzie's a lively one.

MICHAEL. She's not my girlfriend.

AJ. That's all okey-doke so. 'Cos I heard she's shacking up with some movie man across the duck pond.

Michael lunges at AJ with his shovel.

MICHAEL. Lizzie's not that sort!

Mack intervenes.

MACK. Yeah and she's not your girlfriend neither. Don't mind him, son. **Bíodh deoch agat linn.** (Come on have a drink with us.)

Mack thrusts a bottle of whiskey at Michael. Michael shakes his head.

MICHAEL. Tabharfaidh sé an 'sack', dhom. (I'll get the sack.)

AJ. Not a bit of it.

MACK. And isn't every man entitled to the auld tea break.

Michael still refuses the offer of drink.

[threat] Union rules.

Michael drinks and almost chokes. The men let out a raucous cheer.

And wouldn't the tea break be a dull affair without an auld song. What about the auld habitual?

The men launch into McAlpine's Fusiliers.

ALL. I remember the day
That the Bear O'Shea
Fell into a concrete stair
What Horseface said
When he saw him dead
Well it wasn't what the rich call prayers
I'm a navvy short
Was his one retort
That reached unto my ears
When the going is rough
Well you must be tough
With McAlpine's Fusiliers
I've worked till the sweat
Near had me beat
With Russian, Czech and Pole
At shuttering jams
Up in the hydra dams
Or underneath the Thames in a hole
I grafted hard
And I got me cards
And many a ganger's fist across me ears
If you pride your life
Don't join, by Christ
With McAlpine's Fusiliers

They pass the whiskey bottle round as they sing. As the song winds down to a drowsy stop, the men flake out on the sand and fall asleep.

SCENE 10

SANDMAN. In your waking hours you may say what you like. You may swear blind that black is white. But strange and fantastical as they may be, in your dreams you cannot tell a lie.

Michael rises from his slumber. He has walked into a dream. The music of the desert floats over the hollow. He looks up at the high ridge at the top of the sand cliff. Like an angel, Lizzie appears above him on the dune-top. He tries to call out but she doesn't hear, tries to climb the cliff but his legs are like lead. Lizzie disappears from the ridge and Michael's dream disappears. He returns to the sprawl of his drunken sleep. The Gaffer enters. AJ has woken up and gets shovelling. The gaffer points at Mack and Michael.

GAFFER. You two! Get off my site! You're fired! You understand me now, don't you. Go on. Sling your hook!

AJ keeps the head down, working away.

MACK. Well AJ? Are you right?

AJ. I'm right all right. The gaffer's tough, but he's fair. You just can't have lads boozing and snoozing on the job, can you?

Mack lunges at AJ but Michael holds him back.

MICHAEL. Leave him be Mack. We'll be all right. We'll find something else.

Michael and Mack leave, sadly singing McAlpine's Fusiliers.

SCENE 11

Lizzie enters with a basin of water and some dirty shirts. She moves slowly and with sadness.

SANDMAN. 12-month after 12-month. Years pass. Michael is not the only one who can't escape those mocking dreams of love. Just like a mark that won't wash, Lizzie Lavelle can't get Michael out of her mind.

She tries to rub the clothes clean but there's a mark that won't come out. She sings Yolanda's Cuban song but she's close to tears. Granger enters. He throws down a pile of shirts at Lizzie.

GRANGER. Dirty, dirty, dirty. You want to make me a laughing stock? These shirts are not clean. I can't wear these.

Lizzie sings louder.

Yolanda? Yolanda? Hola?

LIZZIE. What have you done to her?

GRANGER. Nada. It's just ... Somebody tipped off the guys in immigration and next thing you know Yolanda's on the next banana boat back to Santo Whatever. It was emotional. But hey, I still have you.

LIZZIE. You don't have me, and you won't have me.

Slowly and menacingly Granger begins to strip off his jacket, then shirt, shoes, trousers and socks. Underneath he's wearing his tight swimming trunks.

GRANGER. Oh come on kid. Give in to it. You know you want to ... be in the movies. And I know that sometimes you fantasize. You wonder what it would be like ... to be a star. Don't you?

Granger kicks the pile of clothes at Lizzie.

Or do you want to be a slave all your life! Have them spotless by tonight, or else ...

He strides off. Lizzie sees a white letter poking from the pocket of Granger's jacket. Lizzie delves into the pocket finding dozens more letters. Lizzie rips them open and scans them in great excitement. Then she finds another bundle of letters in pink envelopes. Excitement turns to anger. She throws Granger's clothes into a pile, tips the dirty washing water over them, and kicks sand over them. She runs off clutching the letters.

SANDMAN. The bastard. All those long years Granger has been waylaying Michael's lonely love letters to Lizzie. Those letters pouring out his shame over not rescuing her like he said, those letters pleading for forgiveness, those letters dancing with the dream that one day they'll be together again. But as Lizzie reads them for the first time, the dates on the letterhead go fewer and farther in between and Michael's copperplate hand crumbles to the scrawl of a child. The last dated correspondence from Lizzie's long-lost lover is just a faded postcard from Brightmouth beach. It reads: Wish you were here. Weather good. Sand terrible. All my love forever, Your Michael.

SCENE 12

A jauntily posh English lady with a old-style pram enters.

LADY. *[to audience]* Splendid weather we're having. We adore the seaside at this time of year, don't we? *[to her baby]* Yes we do. Yes we do ...

In tumbles Michael. Drunk, dishevelled and laden down with dozens of tacky bucket and spade sets. He makes a bee-line for the lady.

MICHAEL. Buckets and spades! Buckets and spades! Get your bucket and spades! Madam! What about a bucket and spade for the child? Great for the sand castles.

LADY. I don't need any.

MICHAEL. I've got buckets of spades and buckets in spades. All the colours of the rainbow. Please.

LADY. *[trying to get away]* Please go away. You're frightening the baby.

MICHAEL. Honest now. The child will have need of a bucket and spade when he grows up big. How's he going to dig the sand?

LADY. I said no. Don't you people understand?!

MICHAEL. I know. I know. I know. I'm a hateful disgrace of a man. I know that. It's just that I have nothing to look forward to. Because all I can do is look back. Because once I had a girl but she doesn't love me anymore and my letters are not replied. And she's like that pinch of sand you can't shake out. That pinch of sand that itches and itches until you're more than positive you're going out of your mind. So please. Buy a bucket, buy a spade. All I need is the price of a drop to make the itch stop.

LADY. Go home! You people. You come over here. Why don't you all go home, go away, go back to where you came from?

The Lady runs off. Michael is on his knees, pouring handful after handful of sand onto his head.

MICHAEL. Mar go bhfuil mé ag dul faoi. (Because I'm sinking). I'm sinking.

SCENE 13

Granger enters talking fancy talk about starlets and movie deals on his mobile phone. He does not see Lizzie Lavelle who enters just behind him.

GRANGER. Wait till you see this kid. Sweet meat, just like you like it ... Oh, I know she'll do it. I've been working on the kid and I think she's just about ready for her big screen debut ... Don't worry, I'll make her an offer she can't refuse.

Lizzie boots Granger in the backside.

GRANGER. What the hell do you think you're doing?

Lizzie brandishes the letters in Granger's face.

LIZZIE. I should ask you the same question you filthy yoke, you. I found your dirty laundry sir.

GRANGER. The letters? Is that what this is about? I was trying to protect you kid, in fact I was doing you a big favour. Your boyfriend sounds like a real jerk.

Lizzie brandishes a bundle of pink letters.

LIZZIE. These aren't poor Michael's letters. I have them read alright. No these are the other ones I found. Addressed to you from a certain lady named ... Trixie Labello. Your girlfriend sounds like a real floozy.

GRANGER. Gimme those!

Granger grabs the letters.

LIZZIE. Help yourself. Those are the tame ones. The raunchy material is safe and sound in the 1st National Bank downtown. I'm sure your wife would love to read them on the way to her divorce lawyer.

GRANGER. Come on kid, I've always been good to you.

Lizzie turns to walk away.

Please. Don't tell my wife, don't tell my wife. I couldn't bear it. She'll take me for every penny I got.

Granger falls to his knees.

Please Lizzie! What do you want?

LIZZIE. Make me an offer I can't refuse. For starters I want a first class ticket back home to Emlyclough. And sure the rest we can sort out on the way to the bank.

Lizzie exits followed by a defeated Granger.

SCENE 14

SANDMAN. At long last Lizzie can see a glimmering of something good on the horizon. **Ní h-amhlaidh do Mhichael é áfach. Michael atá ina shuí ar thrá Bhrightmouth gan ach mian amháin fágtha aige ina shaol – a bheith sé troigh faoin ghainimh gharbh liath sin**. (But not Michael. On Brightmouth beach he sits and grain by grain, he wishes himself seven feet under that shingly sand). But sure there's always hope isn't there?

Mack enters laden down with his own collection of buckets and spades. He's very very drunk.

Isn't there?

He tries to flog them to the audience but he's a stumbling slurring mess. The commotion snaps Michael out of his self pity. He stares wide-eyed at Mack's sorry state.

MACK. Spades of buckets and buckets in spades.

MICHAEL. Mack.

Michael goes to Mack. He tries to make him sober up.

MACK. Spades of buckets and buckets in spades.

MICHAEL. Mack. Stop. You're making a show of yourself!

Michael shakes Mack roughly. Mack pushes Michael away.

MACK. Spades, spades, spades!

Michael tries to grab the buckets and spades.

MICHAEL. Give me them!

MACK. Buckets, buckets, buckets!

Michael tries to grab the merchandise but Mack swings out and Michael gets a face-full of buckets and spades. Michael's blood boils. He takes a swing and floors Mack.

MICHAEL. *[regretful]* Hokey, the roughness of this sand has us set ragged and mean.

MACK. Ladies and gents now please!

MICHAEL. It's too rough for a man like me.

MACK. Have you no home to go to?

Michael makes a decision. He throws away the buckets and spades and helps Mack to his feet.

Time now, ladies and gents. Have you no home to go to?

MICHAEL. Yes Mack. Yes!

Michael runs off towards the Atlantic Ocean.

SCENE 15

SANDMAN. Lizzie Lavelle stepped off a cross-pond liner and onto Brightmouth Beach the very next day. **Ach dé ná deatach ní fhaca sí ar Michael.** (But there was not a sign of Michael). Well. I suppose it was foolish to think that two grains of sand thrown to the wind would ever meet again. But then. People aren't pebbles and don't they have the strangest magnetism for a certain place called home.

Over the hill comes Lizzie – a picture of movie star glamour – black sunglasses, dainty suitcase and all. She looks around to see that the place has changed. There's an echoing tragedy about it.

LIZZIE. Hello? Father? Anyone? I'm back.

Suddenly Michael appears on the other side of the hollow.

MICHAEL. Lizzie Lavelle!

He runs to her.

LIZZIE. Michael Meenaghan!

SLAP! Lizzie hits Michael with a stinger on the left cheek.

LIZZIE. I'm after searching Brightmouth to Whitepool beach and here you were all along.

MICHAEL. I thought you were lost forever, beyond in the Lamptons.

LIZZIE. I might go back. Don't count your chickens.

MICHAEL. No, no, no. Absolutely. I won't.

Lizzie's front evaporates – her heart melted. THEY KISS.

LIZZIE. I love you Michael Meenaghan.

MICHAEL. I love you Lizzie Lavelle.

SCENE 16

Suddenly over the crest of the dune a large Ball comes tumbling down into the hollow. There's a feeble cry and the two teams again come down the slope. They have become old and decrepit.

COMMENTATOR. *[exhausted]* You have us discovered in the dying moments of this quite remarkable fixture. This truly cataclysmic contest has been playing on for months, or is it years, and the pitch here at Emlyclough has, a long while since, been submerged in sand. Cén dochar? Coinneoidh an dá fhoireann seo ag streachailt orthu go dtí'n deireadh. (No matter. These two teams will slug it out to the end). The pitch has sunk in sand, and the fields of Emlyclough north and south have sunk in sand. Cén dochar? 'Sé ár n-oidhreacht é. (What harm? This is sport, this is what we are). The gables of each and every house in Emlyclough has been gobbled alive by sand. Que sera. Níl aon bhaile uathu níos mó. Níl sa saol acu anois ach an cluiche. (This game is their home now). The church was swallowed by sand last week. Be Hokey – Ball is a religion to these people. Elderly relatives, young children, lambs and sheep have been covered with sand. Nach cuma? (Who cares?) It's more important than that. Their mothers, fathers and children have been covered by sand. Good riddance. Let the sand rise. Let it cover pinch by pinch, grain by grain. Céard dhuit'se é? (What is it to you?) This is not your war. Ní raibh tú ann. Ní bhaineann tú linn. Níl aon fháilte romhat anseo. Tá an fuath agat orainn agus an fuath céanna againne ort. (You weren't there, you're not one of us, you don't belong, you hate us and we hate you) – and we hate your ancestors and we'll hate your descendants just the same. If you sink in the sand, I'll sink faster just to spite you. It's a race. It's a game. It's first to the bottom. Under the sand. Seven feet under. In Quicksand. Ach fan go fóill. Tá beirt aghaidh aitheanta i ndiaidh páirt a ghlacadh san iomaíocht. (But hold on, wait a minute. Two familiar faces have joined the fray). None other than the legendary Lizzie Lavelle – and wait – it's Michael Meenaghan, the maestro himself. Agus de réir mar a théann an liathróid árd téann sí fada. Ach meastú cén difríocht a dhéanfaidh an bheirt ionadaí seo don chluiche? (And as the Ball goes long, the Ball goes high. Will these substitutions make a difference?) The Ball goes to Meenaghan. The chance of a lifetime here to finish off the opposition once and for all.

The Ball falls into Michael's hands.

Surely he can score, surely he must. For his family, for his parish and for the blood of his ancestors. *[angry]* Surely he must! He must score! He must! He must! He must!

BANG! Michael punctures the Ball with knife. The players cry out in anger and dismay.

LIZZIE. Enough! **Tá an cluiche thart.** (The game is over).

FATHER. A iníon. M'iníon ó! (Daughter, oh my daughter!)

LIZZIE. It is me, father.

MOTHER. A mhac. Mo mhac ó! (Son, oh my son!)

MICHAEL. It is me, mother.

FATHER+MOTHER. Céard atá ar siúl agaibh? (What are you at?) We're in injury time!

LIZZIE. I'm no daughter of yours unless ye all grow up.

MICHAEL. And I'm no son of yours unless ... Well you know yourselves ... What's the ... Just cop on!

LIZZIE. We're getting married. And you won't stop us this time. Now do you want to be invited to the wedding or not?

FATHER. But we have them nearly bet!

MOTHER. *[to father]* Snail! You may forget that notion! North has the beating of South and you know it.

FATHER. Just give us back the ball and we'll spy who has the beating of who.

MICHAEL. So you won't stand in the way of our marrying?

Mother rips the burst Ball from Michael's hands and boots it up-field. The two teams go hard at it once again. With a war cry the teams chase down the hollow, running out of sight towards the Atlantic. The only ones left in the hollow are Lizzie and Michael.

MICHAEL. *[saddened]* They love the auld game of Ball, don't they?

LIZZIE. *[bitter]* More than anything.

MICHAEL. More than life.

LIZZIE. More than you or me, for certain.

A moment.

MICHAEL. So.

LIZZIE. So. We can't stay here.

MICHAEL. Is there no home for us in Emlyclough?

LIZZIE. There is not. *[beat]* But sure if a person has someone to love then aren't there plenty of places in this wide world to call home? Am I right?

MICHAEL. You're right. *[cheering up]* You're right, Lizzie Lavelle!

Arm in arm, Lizzie and Michael leave the hollow.

SANDMAN. Ba é sin an uair deireadh a leag Lizzie agus Michael súil ar Emlyclough. (That day Lizzie and Michael saw the last of Emlyclough). Off they journeyed to some big city far away. I think it was Belmullet ... but it might have been Dooyork. Anyway, as they quit this sorry place, the game of Ball was in its dying moments. It only lasted another three days. And didn't the score stand at **deich cúl agus naoi gcéad fiche 's a seacht cúilín go Emlyclough Thuaidh. Ocht gcúl, naoi gcéad agus tríocha trí cúilín go Emlyclough Theas.** (Emlyclough North 10 goals and 927 points, Emlyclough South 8 goals and 933 points). Level pegging. But that mighty game never reached its termination. Those two teams were taking their injury rest just here on this spot while the physio attended to PJ Mangan. At least I think he was the one got decapitated. **Cén dochar.** (No matter). So didn't the teams of Emlyclough North and Emlyclough South sit down here for a rest. But with all their enmity, exertion and exhaustion didn't every last one of them fall into the deepest of slumbers. And didn't every last one of them wake up seven feet under the rising sand of Emlyclough. Bequeathing this place to the grass and the moss and the snails and the overhead larks. So you see now don't you? You may forget about your golf ball.

THE NOSE

Based on Nikolai Gogol's story *The Nose*

The Nose premiered at Project Arts Centre, Dublin in November 2008. The play was produced by The Performance Corporation.

Original Cast
Alan Howley
Sonya Kelly
Lisa Lambe
Aongus Óg McAnally
Conan Sweeny
Stephen Swift

Director: Jo Mangan
Set Designer: Ciaran Bagnall
Lighting Designer: Kevin Treacy
Composer: Jack Cawley
Costume Designers: Sinead Cuthbert & Therese McKeone
Choreographer: Nanette Kincaid
Make-up Designer: Lorraine McCrann

SCENE 1

The Major is in the dark.

MAJOR. *[hint of panic]* Father.

[no answer]

Father?

[no answer]

Father, it's Konstantin.

[still no answer]

Where am I? It's dark.

The music of some grotesque revelry emerges.

Oh my God, the ball! I'm late, I'm late, father I'm late and I ...

[beat]

[anxious] I've forgotten something ...

[beat]

The Major finds he is in his underwear

No.

[beat]

My uniform.

The music swells around him in the darkness. Masked figures dance in the gloom as in a Ball.

SCENE 2

A masked figure approaches the Major, sweeps him into a dance.

MAJOR. What's happening?

NOSE. We're having a ball.

MAJOR. Who are you?

NOSE. Isn't it plain Major Kovalyov? *[grabbing his throat, with casual violence]* I'm your nose.

MAJOR. [trying to release her grip] Stop. Stop.

NOSE. No, you stop.

MAJOR. You're choking me.

NOSE. How do you think I feel, I'm your nose.

MAJOR. But it doesn't make sense.

NOSE. *[releasing, perhaps kissing him on the lips]* None of this is going to make much sense.

MAJOR. None of what?

The Nose/Woman exits

Wait. None of what? None of what?!

A bed moves towards The Major, and he's laid down to rest.

Oh, I see! It's all just a bad ... And you're all just figments of my ...

The Major's head hits the pillow, the Ball vanishes and he's fast asleep.

SCENE 3

Clanging church Bells wake The Major with a start.

MAJOR. [waking from nightmare] Agh!

Father, an ancient creature, sits bolt upright beside him in bed.

FATHER. Agh!

MAJOR. What do you think you're doing you old!?

FATHER. There's a man in my bed!

MAJOR. This is my bed.

FATHER. Help!

MAJOR. This is *my* bed!

FATHER. Bed burglar!

MAJOR. *[annoyed]* Father!

FATHER. Father?!

MAJOR. Yes.

FATHER. Who the hell are you calling father!?

MAJOR. I'm your son!

FATHER. Impossible!

MAJOR. Get out.

The Major jumps out of bed, starts to dress, nothing goes on right.

FATHER. *[calling out]* Mother!? Is this one of ours?! Mother where are you?

MAJOR. Mother is ... I said out!

FATHER. My son wouldn't talk to his father like that.

MAJOR. Your son ... *[sees the time]* Ten o'clock! Olga!

FATHER. But my son ... he's such a good little boy. He's a wonderful dancer. He's a prince. He fishes for whales.

MAJOR. [*exasperated*] What?

FATHER. He's a whale fisherman.

MAJOR. *[angry]* Where's my tea!?

FATHER. Who do you think I am, some sort of servant?!

MAJOR. Exactly!

FATHER. What kind of a son ...?

MAJOR. I am a self-made civil servant. I don't ask for sympathy or help, and I don't expect it. So, don't you go looking for special treatment. In this town, everyone pays their way.

FATHER. But you say I'm your father ...?

MAJOR. I'm warning you, St Petersburg is full of Moldovans and Finns who'd do your job for half the money.

FATHER. Money? Money?

MAJOR. *[lying]* Your money's as safe as houses. It's in the bank. *[beat]* OK, the money is gone.

FATHER. Who are you?

MAJOR. If you don't get out of my bed and get to work in three seconds, you're fired. ONE – TWO – THREE! *[Father doesn't move]* That's it! You are fired!

FATHER. You can't fire me, I may be your father!

MAJOR. I just did!

FATHER. Alright then, I'll have a lie-in.

Father lies down. In seconds he's snoring.

SCENE 4

PODTOCHINA. *[off]* Bonjour!

The Major shakes Father, it doesn't wake him.

Bonjour? Anyone home?

MAJOR. Wake up.

PODTOCHINA. *[off]* Bonjour! Major Kovalyov, vous êtes ici?

MAJOR. Just a minute!

PODTOCHINA. *[off]* Major, is that you?

With trousers round his ankles, the Major tugs Father half off the bed. Madame Podotchin enters to find the men in a compromising position.

MAJOR. So this is how you want it, you old bast ...!

PODTOCHINA. Major?

The Major drops Father.

MAJOR. *[explaining]* He's my father ...

PODTOCHINA. I see nothing.

MAJOR. I couldn't get him off the ...

PODTOCHINA. Je vous ai compris. You are a young man ...

MAJOR. Yes ... No!

PODTOCHINA. Major.

MAJOR. I mean I ...

PODTOCHINA. *[hushing him with a raised forefinger, whispers]* Major, let me be franque. You need a wife.

MAJOR. A wife?

PODTOCHINA. *[wolf whistles]* Olga! Vite!

Olga enters at a canter. She wears a diamond choker.

MAJOR. Miss Olga.

Father wakes, crawls from the bed and exits.

OLGA. We're early. I hope it's not inconvenient.

MAJOR. *[lying]* Of course not.

OLGA. *[besotted]* Oh Major.

PODTOCHINA. This weather is simply too heavy! I shall go for a brisk stroll around le bloque.

OLGA. Shall I go with you ...?

PODTOCHINA. *[panicked]* No! [*guides her to the Major*] Reste ici.

Madame Podtochina exits. The Major and Olga are alone together. A moment.

MAJOR. Beautiful.

OLGA. *[blushing]* Major!

MAJOR. Exquisite.

OLGA. Oh Major, stop.

MAJOR. You're all I think of, night and day.

OLGA. Really?

MAJOR. Really.

OLGA. Oh Major, I have a confession to make.

MAJOR. Yes?

OLGA. I ... I too think of only you.

They kiss passionately.

Stop!

MAJOR. But can't you see? I love you!

OLGA. *[crying]* I can't do this. You must know the truth!

MAJOR. Olga?

OLGA. Remember how Maman said I have an average after-tax income of six thousand roubles per annum?

MAJOR. Vaguely ...

OLGA. *[head in hands]* She said you'd never have me if you knew the truth.

MAJOR. *[concerned]* What is it?

OLGA. It's not six thousand roubles. It's six hundred.

MAJOR. Six hundred?

OLGA. We are ruined! Papa blew the family fortune on some stupid ... complex of beautifully appointed luxury dachas overlooking the crystalline waters of the Bulgarian Black Sea! *[cries]*

MAJOR. I see. The whole family fortune?

OLGA. The whole thing was a fake, a scam.

MAJOR. Oh God. This is terribly ... confusing.

OLGA. How could he be so stupid?

MAJOR. Look Olga, *[checks watch]* I have an urgent game of whist with Colonel Smirnov so ...

OLGA. You still love me, don't you?!

MAJOR. Yes but ...

OLGA. *[falling into his arms]* Oh thank God! Maman said you wouldn't love me if I were poor. But I knew you weren't that kind of man. You're not greedy, or vain, or self-centred. You're not obsessed with status, money and power. You're different from the other civil servants!

PODTOCHINA. *[entering]* Mes petits poulets d'amour! Comment ça va?

OLGA. Oui Maman, c'est tout simplement parfait. Le commandant est un homme trés trés chéri.

PODTOCHINA. *[French]* Formidable? You're a busy man Major so let's tie up the loose ends before the Civil Servants' Ball.

OLGA. *[embarrassed]* Maman.

MAJOR. Loose ends?

OLGA. Maman, don't.

PODTOCHINA. Olga! Allez!

OLGA. Oui Maman. [*exits reluctantly, blowing a kiss to the Major*]

PODOTCHINA. Down to business.

MAJOR. Business?

PODTOCHINA. Alors, Olga is a beautiful, fiercely intelligent girl with an income of give or take six thousand roubles.

MAJOR. Madame ...

PODTOCHINA. YOU are an ambitious young civil servant, with dreams of advancement. But a Collegiate Assessor can't hope for success without a wife. Image is everything. So you see, if a man parades up Nevsky Prospect with a beautiful wife on his arm, his nose held high, then as far as St Petersburg is concerned that man is a virile man, a successful man, a man on the up.

MAJOR. Madame ...

PODTOCHINA. But first you must maximise your advantage! You must see to it that your conquest is spoken of in the best society and in the best publications! And how do you achieve this advantage?

MAJOR. Madame Podtochina ...

PODTOCHINA. C'est simple! This coming Saturday at the Civil Servants' Ball you dear Major will, on bended knee, publicly pronounce your love for my beautiful Olga and ask for her hand, in front of all St Petersburg!

MAJOR. Madame Podtochina. Look, I am very fond of Olga and ...

PODTOCHINA. *[exiting quickly]* Excellent. Au revoir! Until Saturday!

MAJOR. Look, these things are never easy to say, but I think we both know my relationship with Olga is purely platonic.

PODTOCHINA. *[glowing]* Quel romantique!

MAJOR. No. Look, I am a self-made civil servant, so I'll be blunt. I am a close friend of Colonel Smirnov – from the Ministry of Building and Profit. And I'm a favourite of Governor Rachkin. It's only a matter of time before I'm promoted to State Counsellor. So you see, I move in a certain milieu, while Olga ...

PODTOCHINA. *[impressed]* Milieu, Olga's favourite.

MAJOR. Madame Podtochina, you misunderstand ...

PODTOCHINA. Perfectly Major, parfaitement. *[exiting]* Olga will be overjoyed!

MAJOR. Madame Podtochina, no!

PODTOCHINA. Until Saturday!

MAJOR. *[grabbing her arm]* Madame Podtochina, I know everything! About your affairs. I will not marry your daughter.

PODTOCHINA. *[cold threat]* Au contraire. I know everything. *[nodding towards the bed]* About your affairs. So you see, you will marry my daughter.

MAJOR. You've got it all wrong!

PODTOCHINA. I know what I saw.

MAJOR. Ask father ... No, don't ... just ...

PODTOCHINA. Remember, image is everything.

MAJOR. This is blackmail!

PODTOCHINA. Not at all dear Major, it's business, simply business. *[exits]*

SCENE 5

The grand home of Governor Rachkin. The Governor enters, opening and reading a telegram with a growing look of annoyance.

RACHKIN. *[angry]* Katerina. *[beat]* Katerina!

Katerina enters.

She is clearly a man dressed as a girl.

KATERINA. Yes papa.

RACHKIN. *[indulgently]* Katerina what have you done to this ... Major Kovalyov?

KATERINA. Major ...?

RACHKIN. Kovalyov. He smiles at me each time he passes me in the Ministry. You don't just smile at a Governor. *[brandishing telegram]* And now this: He's invited himself over!

KATERINA. Oops ...

RACHKIN. Oops what?!

KATERINA. I think he's in love with me.

RACHKIN. Katerina.

KATERINA. It's not my fault!

RACHKIN. Katerina what did you say to him?

KATERINA. Nothing.

RACHKIN. Katerina.

KATERINA. I may have mentioned something about six thousand roubles per annum, after tax.

RACHKIN. Katerina!

KATERINA. IT WAS AN EXPERIMENT!!!

RACHKIN. Yes, yes I know.

KATERINA. Men are just so ... funny.

RACHKIN. *[upset]* Katerina you poor innocent, he's not a man, he's a civil servant!

KATERINA. I WAS BORED!!

RACHKIN. Sweetheart please. I am a governor. You are my treasure, my only child. *[comforts her]* You must be protected from these ... people.

KATERINA *[meekly]* Yes papa.

A knock at the door.

RACHKIN. You must put an end to this.

KATERINA. Yes papa.

The Major enters bowing.

MAJOR. Governor Rachkin. It's an honour to ...

RACHKIN. Humph! *[exiting]*

The Major and Katerina are alone.

A moment.

MAJOR. Beautiful.

KATERINA. *[mock shy]* Major.

MAJOR. Exquisite.

KATERINA. Oh Major, stop.

He kisses her wrist, or is he kissing the diamond bracelet she's wearing.

MAJOR. You are all I think of, night and day.

KATERINA. Really?

MAJOR. Really.

KATERINA. Oh Major. I have a confession to make.

MAJOR. Yes?

KATERINA. *[lying]* I too think of only you.

The Major tries to kiss her. Katerina slaps him.

Stop!

MAJOR. But can't you see? I love you!

KATERINA. I can't do this. You must know the truth!

MAJOR. Yes?

KATERINA. I ... Remember I told you I had an average after-tax income of six thousand roubles per annum.

MAJOR. *[worried]* Yes, I remember.

KATERINA. I lied to you!

MAJOR. Oh God.

KATERINA. It's twelve.

MAJOR. Twelve?

KATERINA. My average after-tax income is twelve thousand roubles per annum.

MAJOR. Katerina!

KATERINA. You mean you don't mind that I'm a silly little rich girl? You still love me?

MAJOR. More than ever.

KATERINA. Oh Major, I'm so happy!

MAJOR. *[drops to his knees]* Katerina! Marry me!

KATERINA. *[sniggering]* Marry?

MAJOR. Yes! Let's elope! Tonight! Just you and me, and your allowance. We'll fly to Paris, and we'll walk together up the Champs Elysées – man and wife!

KATERINA. *[disgusted]* The Champs Elysées?

MAJOR. Well I just thought ... *[clutching at straws]* If a man parades up the Champs Elysées ...

KATERINA. Are you out of your FUCKING MIND?!

MAJOR. Well I ...

KATERINA. *[grabbing his nose]* If you really loved me you'd want it spoken of in the best society and in the best publications! Not paraded in front of foreigners. *[brainwave]* Which is why dear Major, this coming Saturday at the Civil Servants' Ball you will, on bended knee, publicly pronounce your love for me and ask for my hand ...

MAJOR. *[worried]* ... in front of all St Petersburg?

KATERINA. Oh goody! You agree!

MAJOR. OK.

KATERINA. That is all.

MAJOR. That could be complicated ...

KATERINA. *[shooing him]* That is all.

MAJOR. Paris is lovely in the ...

KATERINA. Now.

MAJOR. Look, I'm a self-made ...

KATERINA. Now, now.

MAJOR. ... civil servant and I ...

KATERINA. THAT IS ALL!

MAJOR. *[exiting]* On my knees, on my knees.

SCENE 6

Next morning. The home of Ivan the barber. Ivan snores gently in his bed, cradling a bottle of booze.

IVAN. *[bolt upright, in the horrors]* Agghh!

PRASKOVYA. Ivan! Control yourself, you miserable whinge-bag!

IVAN. Sorry dear I was having this terrible ...

PRASKOVYA. Don't sorry me! You'll wake the Major with your girly-screams.

IVAN. No but ...

MAJOR. *[muffled from upstairs]* Sweet suffering Jesus!

PRASKOVYA. *[to Ivan]* Agh, you're after waking him!

IVAN. Praskovya? Something's wrong.

PRASKOVYA. There's a queue of filthy stubble-mongers out the door and you're half asleep is what's wrong! Eat your roll and get shaving!

Praskovya tosses Ivan a bread roll.

IVAN. Something bad's happening upstairs.

PRASKOVYA. Don't be so fucking stupid!

IVAN. Listen. The Major's in pain.

PRASKOVYA. Of course he's in pain. He's a civil servant. Now quit lazing about! You'd think you were enjoying some sort of unprecedented period of economic prosperity.

IVAN. What?

PRASKOVYA. Just eat your roll and get to work!

IVAN. Praskovya sweetheart, it's hard ...

PRASKOVYA. *[Seething disgust]* Get away from me!

IVAN. My little roll. There's something inside.

PRASKOVYA. Agh!

Ivan pulls a nose from the roll.

IVAN. AGH. !!!

PRASKOVYA. AGGHHH!!!

IVAN. A nose! A nose!

PRASKOVYA. I can see that! Nose Butcher!

IVAN. It's nothing to do with me!

PRASKOVYA. You gibbering turd. You were that pissed you can't remember, can you?

IVAN. *[Pleading]* Praskovya, no.

PRASKOVYA. Who did you shave yesterday?

IVAN. I can't remember.

PRASKOVYA. Were there any complaints? Did you use any extra bandages?

IVAN. *[remembers]* The Major had a little nick on his neck so I just ...

PRASKOVYA The Major! You've gone and lopped off the Major's hooter, you ... gibbering turd!

IVAN. No!

PRASKOVYA. I'll see you hung for this!

IVAN. But he left with his nose still on.

PRASKOVYA. Then whose nose is it?!

IVAN. *[shaking]* I don't know, I don't know, I don't know! *[beat]* Look, I'll just leave it over here in the corner, resting.

PRASKOVYA. Out! Get it out of this house ...

Praskovya exits, chasing Ivan.

[off] I don't give a damn what you do! You can throw it off St Isaac's Bridge for all I care! And then you can throw yourself after it!

SCENE 7

The Major is dressing at his bedside. He is unaware that his nose is gone.

MAJOR. Father! Father, where is my tea!

FATHER. *[off]* Who do you think I am? Your servant!?

MAJOR. Yes! Now hurry up, I'm late for Smirnov.

The Major goes to the mirror. Takes a look. A moment of horror.

SWEET SUFFERING JESUS! My nose is gone!

Father enters, but it doesn't register that his son's nose is gone.

FATHER. What was that?

MAJOR. MY NOSE IS GONE!

FATHER. I see.

MAJOR. Your son's nose disappears and you don't even care.

FATHER. No, no, my son is a Prince.

MAJOR. And I'm the Holy Pope in Rome! *[peeks in mirror, dawning horror]* Oh my God! I will never make Regional Assessor. I'll never own a dacha, or a racehorse, or a speedboat. I am completely and utterly ruined.

FATHER. Good Lord, your nose is gone.

MAJOR. Yes! We've already established that!

FATHER. Yes ... Your Holiness.

MAJOR. *[gritted teeth]* When I said I was the Pope ...

FATHER. Yes Holy Father?

MAJOR. Forget it! Oh my God, the Civil Servants' Ball! This is a nightmare ...! *[brainwave]* That's it ... It's all a dream. Father, punch me!

FATHER. *[terrified]* What ...?

MAJOR. *[shaking Father]* I have to wake up. Punch me!

FATHER. I can't, I can't.

MAJOR. That's an order!

FATHER. I can't punch a Pope.

MAJOR. That's an encyclical, then! Punch me ...! *[SMACK! Father knocks him unconscious.]*

A moment.

FATHER. *[bending over him]* Well?

The Major comes to, finds his nose is still missing.

MAJOR. Aghhh! Get my carriage ready! Whoever's behind this won't get away with it! You don't come in to a man's home and steal his nose from under ... Get my carriage, father!

SCENE 8

In the Major's stables.

MAJOR. Father! Father! I haven't time for this. Where is my carriage?

FATHER. *[entering]* Who are you?

MAJOR. I'm your son, I must to get to the Ministry straight away.

FATHER. I see.

MAJOR. Wait till Smirnov hears about this!

FATHER. I see.

MAJOR. No carriage, no nose. No nose, no marriage. Get it?

FATHER. Your carriage, is it?

MAJOR. Of course, my carriage. Where is it?

FATHER. He took it away.

MAJOR. Who? Who took it away?

FATHER. *[zoned out]* Yes.

MAJOR. Yes? *[beat]* Yes?

FATHER. *[back to earth]* Where's your carriage?

MAJOR. Yes! Where's my carriage? You were about to tell me.

FATHER. Who are you?

MAJOR. I'm your son.

FATHER. No, no, my son is a Prince. He's a wonderful dancer. He fishes for whales.

MAJOR. Father, my carriage is gone.

FATHER. *[horror]* Oh my God, your carriage is gone!

MAJOR. *[stomps in frustration]* No! Oh no, no, no.

FATHER. Oh, before I forget. He took your carriage.

MAJOR. What!? Who did?

FATHER. Said he won it in a game of whist.

MAJOR. Smirnov! The thieving bastard ...!

The shadow of a oddly Nose-like civil servant passes by.

How much worse can it get ...? How much ...?

The Major points towards the shadow of the Nose. He tries to speak but simply can't.

FATHER. What's that? I'm a little deaf.

MAJOR. ...

FATHER. Yes he looks familiar but ...

MAJOR....

FATHER. *[trying to remember]* I never forget a face.

MAJOR. ...

FATHER. It's coming to me.

MAJOR. *[grabbing Father]* IT'S MY BLOODY NOSE!!

FATHER. He's done well for himself.

MAJOR. He's a STATE COUNSELLOR!! My own nose outranks me!

FATHER. Well look at that, he just got a taxi.

MAJOR. NO! This will not stand! Come back! TAXI!

The Major hops in a taxi.

Driver, follow that nose! Faster! I want that nose back in its place! Slap bang between the eyes! Don't spare the horses! Back just above the whiskers! We're losing him! Hold on, he's stopping!

The Major hops out of the taxi.

But ... this is Governor Rachkin's? No!

Katerina appears at the door to greet the Nose.

KATERINA. State Counsellor, do come in!

The Nose enters.

MAJOR. You there! Nose! Talk to me!

The door is slammed in the Major's face. The Major exits in a state of panic.

Police! Police!

SCENE 9

A police interrogation room. Ivan the barber is seated opposite a policeman.

POLICEMAN. *[speaks into recorder, like a roadie]* One. Two. One. Two! t-t-Two! *[beat]* t-t-TWO! *[beat]* T ...!

IVAN. I told you, I was fishing ...

POLICEMAN. Hold on, hold on. TWO! *[presses record button]*

IVAN. I said I was just fishing.

POLICEMAN. *[into recorder]* Suspect admits he was up to something fishy.

IVAN. No ... Fishing off the bridge.

POLICEMAN. Oh, is that right?

IVAN. It's not a crime.

POLICEMAN. You were the only one without a rod!

IVAN. It ... dropped in the river.

POLICEMAN. That, my friend, was not a rod. It was an object. Now start talking.

Ivan maintains a terrified silence.

[into recorder] Suspect maintained suspicious silence.

IVAN. I'm innocent, I'm innocent!

POLICEMAN. Have you ever been in jail, son ...?

IVAN. I didn't do anything.

POLICEMAN. ... Ever shared a cell with a big hairy Moldovan, or a Finn?

IVAN. I'm a barber. I don't know anything.

POLICEMAN. Fair enough. You don't care about your own safety. *[grabbing his neck]* But I could arrange for something very nasty to happen to your wife.

IVAN. *[hopeful]* You could?

POLICEMAN. I snap my fingers and your missus gets thrown in a cell, chained to you.

IVAN. *[terrified]* No! Please!

POLICEMAN. Chained to the ball and chain.

IVAN. Enough! Enough ...!

POLICEMAN. Do you want to play ball?!

IVAN. Yes!

POLICEMAN. I can't hear you.

IVAN. *[meltdown]* Yes ...! Yes ...! I'll tell you everything!

POLICEMAN. *[into recorder]* Suspect confesses the Kirov murder.

IVAN. The Kirov Murder ...!? No ...!

POLICEMAN. I thought you were playing ball!

IVAN. Yes ... yes ... but ...

POLICEMAN. Then tell me what you threw off the bridge!

IVAN. It was a nose! It was a nose! That's all I knows!

POLICEMAN. *[into recorder]* Suspect confesses ... A nose? Come on! That doesn't make sense!

IVAN. I know!

POLICEMAN. You threw a nose off St Isaac's bridge?

IVAN. I found it in my bread roll. So ... baker's your man!

POLICEMAN. *[sighs, switches off the recorder]*

IVAN. Aren't you going to ...? *[leans towards recorder]* Suspect suspects the baker.

POLICEMAN. Twenty Roubles.

IVAN. What?

POLICEMAN. OK, fifteen.

IVAN. What?

POLICEMAN. I'm a policeman. I can barely pay the rent.

IVAN. *[appalled]* This is incredible.

POLICEMAN. I know, but tell it to the Tsar and you think he'd listen? *[beat]* Fifteen roubles and you walk free, case closed.

IVAN. You're closing the case? What about the nose?

POLICEMAN. Fifteen, I'm not budging from fifteen!

IVAN. But there's a nose butcher on the loose!

POLICEMAN. And I suppose you'd like me to set up some kind of nose squad, or a missing noses bureau? Look, the crime hasn't been reported, therefore it does not exist. Anyway, we both know the story: one scumbag knocking off some other scumbag's nose. As long as it doesn't affect ordinary decent people like policemen, why bother?

IVAN. So you're refusing to investigate.

POLICEMAN. Wouldn't you rather the police were out there catching rapists?

IVAN. But you don't catch rapists!

POLICEMAN. Listen to yourself! Does the environment mean nothing to you? Think about the paperwork on a case like this. Over a nose which may, or may not, have been thrown off a bridge. I mean how do I even know you're telling the truth?

IVAN. Why would I lie about a thing like that?

POLICEMAN. Ten roubles, final offer.

IVAN. It's the truth! You couldn't make it up. It's ridiculous!

POLICEMAN. Five roubles! Five is my absolute final offer!

IVAN. That's fair. That's a fair price. *[hands over five roubles]*

POLICEMAN. Get out of here.

IVAN. Do I get a receipt?

POLICEMAN. Out!

Ivan exits pursued by Policeman.

SCENE 10

The bustling small ads office of the St Petersburg Chronicle. Crowds of customers brandish their ads. The Major forces his way through to the personal ads desk.

CLERK. Next! Your ad please, sir.

MAJOR. *[confidential]* Look, I'm the victim of a vicious practical joke. He's disappeared. I'm offering a substantial reward to whoever brings the bastard back to me.

CLERK. Name please.

MAJOR. We've got to keep this hush-hush.

CLERK. You're placing a small ad, in a newspaper sir.

MAJOR. I can't give my name. Just put respectable civil servant. No, put Major.

CLERK. So this missing person. What is he, a household serf?

MAJOR. A serf? No! *[hushed, embarrassed]* It's my ... my nose.

CLERK. *[scribbling details]* Major offers reward for a Mister Nose ...

MAJOR. No, no, it's my own nose that has disappeared.

CLERK. Yeah, yeah, I get it. But how exactly did he go missing?

MAJOR. Well, I don't know! Look, he's running round town without me, and he's been promoted to State Counsellor.

CLERK. Ah, so this chap's not a serf, he's a State Counsellor.

MAJOR. Exactly!

CLERK. *[grimacing]* Tricky.

MAJOR. What?

CLERK. Tricky.

MAJOR. I'm invited to the Civil Servants' Ball!

CLERK. Yeah, yeah I get it but I can't ...

MAJOR. You've got to help me, it's a matter of life and death!

CLERK. Yeah, yeah I get it. But I don't want to end up in the libel court over this.

MAJOR. What?

CLERK. The Chronicle deals in facts not truth.

MAJOR. But I am telling you the truth!

CLERK. You see? There's your problem. A fact is something that'll stand up in a court of law, whereas the truth is ... Tricky.

MAJOR. But this is madness!

CLERK. *[delighted]* I know, isn't it! Last month a civil servant placed an ad here seeking a 'runaway black poodle'. What was he up to?

MAJOR. ?

CLERK. The whole thing was a satire, on a Sergeant in the Railroad Ministry. The whole thing ended up in court. See? We have to be very careful.

MAJOR. I want to place an ad about my nose, not a poodle!

CLERK. Yeah, yeah I get it, but no.

MAJOR. Please. I have lost my nose.

CLERK. Ah, I get it! You've lost your nose!

MAJOR. And that's why I've got to place this ad.

CLERK. Tricky.

MAJOR. What do you mean tricky?

CLERK. One word, Health and safety. Last month a civil servant placed an ad for a missing Siamese kitten. What happened? It scratched out the eye of a Major in the Mining Ministry. The whole thing ended up in ...

MAJOR. *[revealing his face]* LOOK!

CLERK. *[retching]* Sweet suffering Jesus.

MAJOR. Now will you publish my ad?

CLERK. Flat as a pancake, no denying.

MAJOR. So?

CLERK. Tricky.

MAJOR. ???

CLERK. Think of the children, it's a family newspaper. Last month a civil servant placed an ad for a man-eating Siberian tiger ...

MAJOR. I know, I know, I know. I just want to place an ad!

CLERK. *[peeved]* Yeah, yeah, I get it.

MAJOR. So what am I supposed to do?

CLERK. Try the Baltic News of the World, they're always looking for freaks.

MAJOR. *[grabbing Clerk's lapels]* I am not a freak!

CLERK. *[peeved]* Sorry. Just being helpful.

MAJOR. I'm a collegiate assessor, a Major. I have no nose. *[turns away, cries quietly]*

CLERK. *[sympathetic]* Yeah, yeah, I get it. Must be terribly tricky. But look, life's not so bad, is it? *[offering him snuff]* Here, pinch of snuff?

MAJOR. You bastard!

The Major storms off.

CLERK. Tricky customer.

SCENE 11

The Major walks the brash uncaring streets of St Petersburg. He is buffetted and bruised as he battles against the tide of St Petersburg's busy and self-interested citizens. Finally the Major enters the hallowed refuge of the Kazan Cathedral. He falls to his knees, crosses himself and prays fervently.

MAJOR. Forgive me Lord, forgive me for I have sinned. Lord, show me the error of my ways. Show me ... *[sudden anger]* What did I do to deserve this! [regaining composure] Sorry. Sorry. I'm sorry about that Lord, forgive me. But just tell me this Lord. Was I vain, was I selfish, was I unkind? *[beat]* Look, <u>if</u> I was you know I'll change. I'll be humble and honest and good if you'll only answer this prayer. Lord, return my nose ... to me...

The Major becomes aware of a nasal drone. He spots the shadow of The Nose praying at the far end of the Cathedral. The Major approaches nervously.

[whispers] Sir? Sir? Yes you. *[beat]* I saw you here and ... *[nervous laugh]* I've never done this sort of thing before ... I don't know how to put this ... let's go home together. I need you ... When you went away ... a little part of me died. *[beat]* Don't you understand? I'm a

Major. I shouldn't have to walk around without a nose. It's OK for a beggar to go round without one, it's good for business. But for a civil servant, it's frowned upon. *[beat]* What do you mean you don't understand? Don't play the innocent with me. It's obvious ... It's as plain as the ... *[too loud]* YOU'RE MY NOSE. *[whispers]* You sir, are my nose and you've put me in an impossible situation. The Civil Servants' Ball is on Saturday, did that slip your tiny nasal mind? Katerina, Governor Rachkin's daughter? 12 grand per annum, after tax? Any of this ring a bell? Oh, I suppose that's not good enough for you, State Counsellor. Well, I'm here to tell you that I'm not going to take this anymore. If you were an ear, I might have let it pass but when a nose ups and leaves without a word of explanation, that sir is a crime! A CRIME!

The cathedral is filled with a murmur of indignation. Madame Podtochina appears. The shadow of The Nose vanishes.

PODTOCHINA. *[innuendo]* A friend of yours, Major?

MAJOR. *[flustered, covering his non-nose with a hanky]* Madame Podtochina.

PODTOCHINA. You can't hide behind a handkerchief Major. I see everything. You and your petit ami?

MAJOR. No! No, he's my ... he's a...

PODTOCHINA. Think of poor Olga.

MAJOR. But he's ... it's not like that!

PODTOCHINA. I understand.

MAJOR. Look Madame Podtochina, I can't do this anymore. I can't do it to Olga. I've got to come clean ... *[blurts out]* There's someone else.

PODTOCHINA. *[taken aback]* Major ... I am une femme moderne. As long as you, and the gentleman are discreet I won't say a word.

MAJOR. No! No! You have it all wrong, you see ...

PODTOCHINA. What on earth is the matter with your nose?

MAJOR. *[backing away]* Ha ha ha ha! My nose, what do you mean, my nose? My nose is ... *[realizes Nose has left the Cathedral]* My nose is gone!

The Major runs off in pursuit.

Come back! I need you!

SCENE 12

The sound of an anxious, restless crowd. A TV reporter stands, finger on earpiece, waiting to go live.

REPORTER. Yuri, I'm coming to you live and exclusive from St Petersburg where the city of dreams, has become the city of fear. Yuri, I am here, live, at the Kazan Cathedral where what I can only describe as, a crowd has gathered, live. A crowd of people. A crowd of live people in search of a nose – Yuri.

Places finger to his earpiece to hear the news anchor's question. Short question.

Yuri, you're absolutely right. This doesn't make much sense. No sense does it make, at all. But having said all that, I must tell you that in all my years, since the beginning of my multi-award-winning career, I have *never* covered a story quite like this. Yuri. *[Short question]* I'm sorry Yuri, I didn't quite ... No I've lost audio on this end but I imagine you're asking me to fill time to the ad break, so let me recap on events so far in this extraordinary live and exclusive breaking story, live. Now obviously details are sketchy, and facts are limited but I can reveal this much – There are rumours. Quite what it means we're still unsure but one thing seems almost certain and it's this – a nose has left the face of a civil servant ... Hold on! I think something's happening!

The Major enters, despondent. Beckoning the camera to follow, the Reporter runs in the opposite direction. The Major exits.

Something's happening, something's happening live, live and exclusive ... No. No. Absolutely nothing. Well that's what happens sometimes. Nothing. But as you can probably tell, things here are incredibly tense. As you can see – People are scared. People are scared about losing their own noses, they're scared a nose might come in and take their job. Already I'm hearing utterly unconfirmed reports that some people are keeping their noses indoors for fear of a repeat attack, while others are simply keeping their noses out of other people's business. So you can see that the implications of this story could be huge. What they are we don't know. Only time will tell. For now we can only guess ... as we lie all alone in bed at night, not able to sleep, all we can do is stare at the ceiling, and guess. Yuri. *[A question]* Absolutely Yuri. I know that some commentators are even suggesting that this entire phenomenon, this event, this news-story-of-the-century, call it what you will, is a farce or even a satire on something or other. Not so. I can tell you now that I've been talking to my contacts, I've been talking to my contacts in burnt-out phone-boxes, in underground carparks, on rusty park benches and they are completely and utterly denying any such suggestion. And keep in mind these are people very very close to the source of this unsubstantiated hearsay. *[Short question]* Look. Yuri. *[irritated]* I'm a reporter, I'm a multi-award-winning reporter and I'm here, live. At the end of the day this is my story, understand. I made it, I own it. You can have all the facts and figures you want but you're not here, live. This is having a very real impact on ordinary people, ordinary people like nurses, and policemen. You have no idea what it's like, you have no idea what it's like to be this man *[points at audience member]*. Look at him. He's hurting. Hurting very badly. Trying to keep his family, his home, his very nose above water! How must he be feeling? How must any of these very ordinary people be feeling, right now, live. *[emotional]* Look at them. Look at them! God Bless You! You're all heroes! Heroes! Yuri, back to you in the studio.

SCENE 13

The Major's home. The Major staggers in with a vodka bottle. He's a mess. The TV news is on. The Major switches it off.

MAJOR. There is no hope.

FATHER. ?

MAJOR. My life is over.

FATHER. ?

MAJOR. I can't go out. I can't go to work. I'm finished, understand?

FATHER. ?

MAJOR. And you. You don't even care.

A loud BANGING on the door. The policeman strides in. Father rushes towards him.

FATHER. Thank God, you've come officer! I've been worried sick.

POLICEMAN. *[suspicious]* Is that right?

FATHER. *[clinging to Policeman]* My little boy has disappeared. Something terrible's happened.

POLICEMAN. Suspect is obstructing police business.

FATHER. But my son's gone missing!

MAJOR. I am not missing.

FATHER. Who are you?

MAJOR. *[grabs father, shakes him]* How many times! How many! Look at me! LOOK at me! I am your son! Look at my face, I know you know me! *[upset, regretful]* So why can't you just remember, just once? Father, please.

POLICEMAN. *[roughly grabbing father]* Suspect is wasting police time!

MAJOR. *[grabbing father back]* How dare you treat an old man like that! Who do you think you are?! And why aren't you out there catching rapists? What the hell do you want!?

POLICEMAN. Am I addressing Major Kovalyev?

MAJOR. Yes ... Why?

POLICEMAN. We got him.

MAJOR. Him?

POLICEMAN. Your nose.

MAJOR. *[embracing him]* Oh thank God! Thank God!

POLICEMAN. Following a city-wide investigation involving members of the newly formed Nose Squad and The Missing Noses Bureau we caught your nose trying to board a stagecoach to Moscow. And get this, he was trying pass himself off as a State Counsellor.

The policeman holds up a nose.

MAJOR. Thank you! Thank you! How can I ever thank you!?

POLICEMAN. Fifty roubles.

MAJOR. What?

POLICEMAN. Fifty roubles.

MAJOR. You want fifty roubles?!

POLICEMAN. Call it forty. No questions asked.

MAJOR. *[appalled]* Incredible.

POLICEMAN. I know. The going rate's eighty. I'm a policeman.

MAJOR. *[thrusting the cash at him]* There! Take it!

POLICEMAN. Do you want a receipt?

MAJOR. Just my nose, thank you!

The Major grabs the nose. Policeman exits. The Major dances his nose round the room.

I shall go to the ball!

He pauses, then presses nose to his face.

Look at me now! Just look at me now!

The nose drops off. It won't stay on.

FATHER. My.

MAJOR. NO! NO! NO! *[exits running]* Help! Help!

SCENE 14

The Major is waylaid by a manic crew of paramedics who lift him onto a trolley/ambulance and wheel him at break neck speed through the city, removing his watch and wallet as they distract him with oxygen mask and other such emergency treatments.

The trolley 'crash-lands' in an operating theatre. A surgeon and a nurse enter, ready to operate on the Major, now completely hidden by a surgical cover.

SURGEON. It's natural to be nervous Nurse Relkova. Everyone's nervous their first time working in theatre ... especially actors.

NURSE. ??

SURGEON. Ha ha ha, my little icebreaker.

NURSE. Ha ...

SURGEON. Relax nurse, relax. It's not like it's a matter of life or death. Scalpel!

MAJOR. *[weak, from under cover]* Hello?

NURSE. *[flustered]* Scalpel. Scalpel.

MAJOR. Hello? *[The surgeon cuts]* Agghhh!

SURGEON. Hammer!

NURSE. Hammer.

BANG! The surgeon knocks the Major out.

SURGEON. Nose!

NURSE. Nose.

SURGEON. Sewing kit!

NURSE. Sewing kit? *[she hands it over, confused]*

SURGEON. Give me vitals on the nose, nurse!

NURSE. The BP's one hundred, the pulse is strong.

SURGEON. Damn it nurse!

NURSE. What?!

SURGEON. We're out of white thread! OK, I'll go with the beige.

The surgeon positions the nose the wrong way up on the Major's face.

There we go, more handsome already.

NURSE. Um ... The nostrils usually go just above the mouth doctor.

SURGEON. Oops-a-daisy. You know nurse, for him that's a better look. And you know something else? I'm going to go with my first instinct. The beige thread is just wrong. Arc welder!

NURSE. Arc ...? Arc Welder?!

SURGEON. Do you want to cure this nose or not?!

The nurse hands over the welder and sparks fly.

Now we're talking. Who's afraid of a bit of singeing?

The surgeon sings a jaunty pop song as black smoke rises from the operating table. The Nose monitor goes into overdrive.

NURSE. Stop! Doctor you've got to stop!

SURGEON. Don't panic! Don't panic!

NURSE. We're losing him! We're losing the nose!

SURGEON. He's heat sensitive, that's all!

There's an explosion and the Nose monitor flat lines.

[perplexed] Well ... I was not expecting that. *[business like]* Bag him up nurse, and grab yourself a coffee. *[nurse goes to exit]* And nurse, don't blame yourself. What happened here today was *not* your fault.

Nurse exits. Surgeon takes out a phone.

[into phone] Svetlana, get Nurse Relkova's P45 ready, good girl.

Rattles the trolley to wake the Major.

Wakey, wakey. You're not in Kansas anymore! Major!

MAJOR. *[under covers]* Ugghhhhh...

SURGEON. *[to the head of the trolley]* Major!!

MAJOR. *[raising head from opposite end]* Ugghhhh ... What?

SURGEON. Major, your nose fought very, very hard. But in the end it was ... it was my theatre nurse ... the worst case of negligence I've seen in thirty years. Had to give her the old heave-ho.

The Major emits a sob.

Oh, don't feel bad for her, Major. You've got to weed out the bad apples.

MAJOR. What about my nose? Is there really no hope?

SURGEON. Oh, I would never say that ... Except in this case. *[shunting Major off the trolley]* Do you mind?

MAJOR. God! Why don't I just throw myself off St Isaac's bridge!

SURGEON. Why not. But you wouldn't mind settling up with Svetlana in accounts first? A cheque is fine.

MAJOR. You bastard! You killed my nose and now you want a cheque!?

SURGEON. Cash is good. *[beat]* I understand, you're upset. But you know what they say – Miracles happen. Of course they never do, but that's what they say. *[throws him the bagged-up nose]* Here you go.

SCENE 15

The Major's bedroom. The sound of church bells. The Major is in bed, hiding himself under the covers. Father enters waving The Baltic News of the World.

FATHER. It doesn't make sense. I don't understand.

MAJOR. *[under the covers]* Go away.

FATHER. There is an article in the newspaper.

MAJOR. Please father, not now.

FATHER. *[worried]* It says here some civil servant's gone and lost his nose. Poor devil.

MAJOR. *[warning]* Father ...

FATHER. *[reads headline]* 'Rachkin's nose out of joint over faceless bureaucrat'. Governor Rachkin is snorting mad over reports that a flat-faced functionary will steal the limelight from under his nose at tonight's Civil Servants' Ball.

MAJOR. Father!

FATHER. The nose job sparked a flurry of trunk calls to Moscow. But the Ministry is playing down the story, claiming the nose has been blown, out of all proportion ...

MAJOR. Father! It's me!

The Major sits up in bed. His nose has returned.

I am the nose-less civil servant, remember?!

FATHER. OK ... whoever you are.

MAJOR. Rachkin won't see his beakless bureaucrat tonight. I'm never leaving this house again.

FATHER. *[exiting]* By the way, you've got a spot.

The Major touches his face and feels a nose. The Major finds a mirror, slowly brings it to his face.

AH!!! AHA HAAA!!!!!! AHAHAAAAA!!!!! YOU'RE BACK!

[entering] Who's back?

MAJOR. My nose! My nose is back! I've been given a second chance – a chance to start again.

Dancing Father around the bedroom.

FATHER. *[faint glimmer]* I know you ...

MAJOR. A chance to make some serious money!

FATHER. *[the glimmer dies]* No.

MAJOR. Katerina here I come!

The Major grabs his uniform jacket and exits. Father goes back to his newspaper.

SCENE 16

The Civil Servants' Ball is well underway. Katerina and her father Governor Rachkin are in pride of place. The Major dashes in, out of breath. He is about to move toward Katerina when Madame Podtochina looms out of nowhere and dances him away.

PODTOCHINA. *[delight]* Major!

MAJOR. *[muted horror]* Madame Podtochina!

PODTOCHINA. You're late, Major dear. Olga was worried.

MAJOR. Oh God.

PODTOCHINA. Major, you're nervous.

MAJOR. Yes I'm ...

PODTOCHINA. Moi aussi!

MAJOR. Madame Podtochina, I've ...

PODTOCHINA. Well? Have you got the ring?

MAJOR. Yes I have a ring but ...

PODTOCHINA. Quelle joie! *[pulling him to her breast]* To have you as a son!

MAJOR. Madame Podtochina, Olga is a lovely girl and I ...

PODTOCHINA. Isn't she stunning?!

MAJOR. Yes but ...

Madame Podtochina spins the Major to Olga, they dance.

PODTOCHINA. Fly lovebirds, fly!

Madame Podtochina dances with Governor Rachkin, they talk and nod, looking in the direction of The Major and Olga.

OLGA. Darling!

MAJOR. *[regretful]* Oh, Olga.

OLGA. Darling, I was worried.

MAJOR. Really?

OLGA. The last time we met you seemed a little ...

MAJOR. Olga, Look, I ...

OLGA. Look, I love you. That's all.

MAJOR. *[nauseous]* Oh God, Olga this is very difficult ... *[she hushes him]*

OLGA. Major, my mother loves grand gestures but that's not me. If you want to ask me discreetly, I don't mind. What do *you* want Major?

MAJOR. What do I want ... No you see...

OLGA. What?

MAJOR. I want a drink.

The Major rushes off. His path is blocked by Governor Rachkin.

RACHKIN. Major Kovalyov! A little bird tells me we may have an announcement here tonight.

Governor Rachkin points out Olga. But the Major misunderstands he's pointing out his daughter Katerina.

MAJOR. *[surprised, looking towards Katerina]* Oh. Well yes, Governor Rachkin, sir. I hope so.

RACHKIN. I am delighted. She really is a lovely girl.

MAJOR. Well, you should know.

RACHKIN. What?

MAJOR. *[staring at Katerina]* I'm so happy to have your approval.

RACHKIN. It's nothing to do with me. Her mother wears the trousers.

MAJOR. [still focussed on Katerina] She does?

RACHKIN. But she's all for it.

MAJOR. She is?

RACHKIN. Well? What are you waiting for?

MAJOR. Yes, what am I waiting for? Thanks ... Dad.

RACHKIN. ???

The Major rushes to Katerina, falls to his knees, a hush descends.

MAJOR. Katerina! You said you wanted me on me knees in front of all St Petersburg. Well, here I am!

KATERINA. I said that?

MAJOR. Katerina, I love you with all my heart.

KATERINA. Oh dear.

MAJOR. Will you marry me?

KATERINA. Come again?

MAJOR. Marry me?

KATERINA. Ohhh-Kayyyy. You know Colonel Smirnov, don't you? *[displaying a big diamond ring]* My fiancée.

Smirnov steps forward and smugly takes Katerina's hand.

MAJOR. Your fiancée? But Katerina! You insisted, you told me to ask for your hand in front of all St Petersburg.

KATERINA. I did?

MAJOR. Yes!

KATERINA. Yeah, well ... that was ages ago.

MAJOR. It was Tuesday!

KATERINA. People change, Major. And anyway ... [laughs patronizingly, others laugh along]

MAJOR. Anyway what?

KATERINA. Isn't it obvious Major? I mean, look at you. It's as plain as the nose on your face.

MAJOR. It ... was you!

KATERINA. *[perplexed]* I'm sorry?

MAJOR. You and my nose were in cahoots!

KATERINA. Your nose?

MAJOR. This is just typical of you people! Playing sick jokes on civil servants for fun!

KATERINA. Do you know who you're talking to?

MAJOR. Stealing a man's nose is a crime! It's nose burglary!

KATERINA. *[furious]* DO YOU KNOW WHO YOU'RE TALKING TO?!

MAJOR. To be honest, I haven't a clue! I mean ... LOOK! ...YOU'RE NOT EVEN A GIRL!

A cry of mass indignation. Katerina rushes off in tears. Governor Rachkin storms up to the Major, floors him with a punch.

RACHKIN. You're fired!

PODTOCHINA. I never liked you! *[kicks him]*

Olga storms up to the Major.

OLGA. !!!

Olga turns to run, wheels back around.

What was I thinking!? You *are* that kind of man. Greedy and vain and self-centred. Just like all the other civil servants!

MAJOR. Olga.

OLGA. Goodbye Major.

Olga departs. The glamour of the ball unravels around The Major.

MAJOR. Olga! OLGA!

SCENE 17

Utterly alone, the Major sets off on the long dark walk home against the cold winter wind and rain. As he trudges on, he rips off his Collegiate Assessors jacket, kicks it away. He arrives home. The Major is in the dark. Half-dressed and close to tears.

MAJOR. *[weakly]* Father?

Father jumps up in the bed, half-asleep.

FATHER. Where's my son?! What have you done with him!?

MAJOR. I'm taking him down to St Isaac's Bridge and I'm going to throw him off.

FATHER. Murderer!

MAJOR. He's a little bastard.

FATHER. You take that back!

MAJOR. He's a stupid, selfish bastard who deserves everything he gets.

FATHER. My son is a good boy!

MAJOR. *[close to tears]* I'm sorry, but he's not. He's going to go now. He just wanted to say ... goodbye.

FATHER. *[the fog finally lifting]* Hold on a minute! You ... you're Konstantin. My son Konstantin! *[embracing the Major]* You came back to me, after all these years!

MAJOR. Father, I'm sorry.

FATHER. What are you sorry for?

MAJOR. Everything.

Gentle waltz music plays.

FATHER. Forget about it. Let's break out the booze!

Father opens a bottle of vodka and they drink a toast.

Long life and happiness!

MAJOR. I am a terrible son.

FATHER. What? You're the best son a man could have.

MAJOR. How could I be? I treated you like a slave. I cheated you out of everything you ever worked for ...

FATHER. But think of the memories we have!

MAJOR. You have memories?

FATHER. Don't you remember? When you were a little boy, we used to go fishing.

MAJOR. Fishing?

FATHER. Off St Isaac's Bridge.

MAJOR. Yes. *[laughing]* Fishing for whales. You said we were whale fishermen!

FATHER. *[indicates a small fish]* The size of them. Mother used to laugh.

MAJOR. Mother.

FATHER. Your poor mother. When you were little, she would call you her Prince, her little Prince. Remember?

MAJOR. Yes, father.

Father embraces the Major. They start to dance a waltz.

FATHER. And you used to dance with her. You were a wonderful dancer. And every night we'd have a ball ...

MAJOR. In the kitchen.

FATHER. Right here. In the kitchen.

The dance continues as the light slowly fades.

MAJOR. We had a ball.

FATHER. Yes.

MAJOR. Yes, father. Yes. We had a ball.

POWER POINT

Author's Note

Power Point is a site-specific play written for the business conference room at the Camden Court Hotel, Dublin. The character of Sonny should be played by a woman or an older man, or anyone that the audience will find it hard to believe is the biological son of Jack and Jill.

Power Point premiered in September 2009 at Dublin's Absolut Fringe festival. The play was produced by The Performance Corporation. In August 2010, the play was presented at the Tampere Theatre Festival in Finland.

Original Cast

Mary: Clare Barrett
Jack: Alan Howley
Jill: Lisa Lambe
Sonny: Hilary O'Shaughnessy

Director: Jo Mangan
Set and Lighting Designer: Ciaran Bagnall
Costume Designer: Suzanne Keogh

The audience enters the conference room of the hotel.

MARY, the conference organizer, enters.

MARY. Hello.
Hello.
Welcome.
Before we get down to business, a small bit of housekeeping.
You all know why we're here.
You all know what this is about.
We're here, because you're here.
If you weren't here ...
Where would we be?
Moving on.
Introductions.
I am delighted ...
We are delighted.
As are they.
You are particularly, I'm sure.
But just to put it in context.
There are rocks.
Winds, backing south-southwest.
Gale force ten.
We are taking on water.
We are in troubled waters.
Troubled waters which are uncharted.
No map.
It went overboard.
As I said, there are rocks.
And the lighthouse keeper is on fire.
But these are mere metaphors.
It's all hands on deck.
Don't you agree?
You know where I'm coming from?
We are where we are.
We live in baffled times.
That much is standard-issue.
And knowledge is, by definition, unknowable at the best of times.
Hindsight is the soul of convenience.
Well, that's how I was brought up.
But let us not dwell in the present.
Let us not look forward.

Let us look both ways before crossing the road.
Juggernauts carry heavy loads.
Lorries come out of nowhere.
When was the last time the brakes were checked?
Like so many runaway trains, you're thinking.
It's all over in a flash.
And you'll be a long time dead.
But it's not all doom and ...
Wild horses never refused oats.
I think it's something we should keep in mind throughout.
So what approach do we take?
Do donkeys want carrots?
Or should they stick to their guns?
Which brings me neatly to the same place.
We have here two people.
They speak for themselves.
And I know you'll find their perspective is both invaluable and nebulous.
Certainly, wherever they speak they provoke lively debates.
And so, without further ado.
Put your hands in the air.

MARY encourages polite applause.

Yes. Please. Thank you.

JACK and JILL enter the room, accepting the audience's applause.

JACK. Hello.

JILL. Congratulations!

JACK. We're all here.

JILL. You made it!

JACK. Give yourself a slap in the face.
Now we're in business!
But let me ask you a question.
What are we in business for?
Why do we do what we do?
What motivates us?
What?

JILL. Profit? Passion? People?

JACK. All the P's...

JILL. Principles? Power? Posterity?

JACK. In other words what is business all about?

JILL. Anyone?

JACK. Let me put it another way.
Hands up who feels happy.
Hands up who feels sad.
Hands up who feels absolutely nothing at all.
Good.

JACK. Now we know where we stand.
Hands up who feels that happiness is more important than money.
Hands up who feels that family is more important than career.
Hands up who feels that life is more important than death.
Hands up who'd sell their soul for a rasher sandwich.
Hands up.
Hands up who has regrets.
Hands up who has no regrets.
Hands up who's deluding themselves.
Hands up who's deluding themselves, but can't admit it.
Hands up who admits to deluding themselves but wants us to think they're living in blissful ignorance.
Hands up.
Hands up who lives in a greenhouse.
Hands up who threw stones.
Hands up who stole apples.
Hands up who judged a book by its cover.
Hands up who mitched off religion.
Hands up.
Hands up who made that phone call on the fateful night in question.
Hands up who picked up the phone, dialled the number, then hung up.
Hands up who picked up the phone, dialled the number and said...

JILL. Jesus? Is that you?

JACK. Hands up.

JILL. *[perhaps aimed at JACK]* Hands up who believes that bad things happen when good men fail to act.
Hands up who believes that good things happen when bad men fail to act.
Hands up who believes that good women act when bad men fail to happen.
Hands up.

JACK. Hands up who's living the dream.
Hands up whose life has become a living nightmare with no end in sight.
Hands up who lives for Friday.
Hands up who wants to live forever.
Hands up who just died and went to heaven.
Hands up.

JILL. Hands up who hates pain.
Hands up who loves pain.
Hands up who believes pain is all in the head.
Hands up who believes life is a kick in the head.
Hands up.

JACK. Hands up who believes the truth shall set us free.
Hands up who thinks seeing is believing.
Hands up who can barely believe their eyes.
Hands up who thinks, you know what, the proof is in the pudding.
Hands up.
Good.
This is business.
We are business people.
Crisis, what crisis?
Hands up!

JILL. Hands up who's willing to sacrifice it all for an idea.
Hands up who's willing to sacrifice it all for just one moment of existential bliss.
Hands up who's willing to sacrifice it all for a three-bed apartment with sea views.

JACK. Hands up who likes puppies.

JILL. Hands up.

JACK. *[grabbing Mary]* HANDS UP AND NO ONE GETS HURT!

Joke ... joking ...

JILL. *[at JACK]* Hands up who sometimes wonders.
Hands up who sometimes despairs.
Hands up who sometimes ...

JACK. Hands up who is prepared to forgive.
Hands up who is prepared to forgive but not forget.
Hands up who agrees with the statement ...

JILL. We live in unprecedented times.

JACK. Hands up who disagrees with the statement ...

JILL. We live in unprecedented times.

JACK. Hands up who thinks the statement ...

JILL. We live in unprecedented times.

JACK. Is nonsense because after all, tomorrow is another day.
Or is it?
The figures don't add up.
The bottom has fallen out of the market.
Are you even listening?
Can you believe what you're seeing?
Good.
We're getting somewhere.
Very Good.
We're getting nowhere, fast.
Where was I? Where am I?
Are you with me at the back!?
Yes, I hear you.
You want strategies.
You want answers.
You are panicking.
I can see it in your frightened little eyes.
You're looking at me with your eyes and you're asking ...
How are we going to get out of this?
WELL I DON'T KNOW!

I'm totally and utterly clueless!
Still panicking?
GOOD.
Because do you know what?

PANIC is the NUMBER ONE tool for SUCCESS in business today.
God I love a crisis!
I fucking LOVE IT, man.
Don't you?
It makes us feel ... special.
It makes us feel like we are alive.
It makes us feel like we're the beating centre of the universe.
It makes us feel like what we think really matters.
And that, my friends, is good for business.

Pause.

Let me just for a moment tell you a story ...

A long time ago I was on my way home, stuck in the most terrible traffic jam you can imagine and I just turned to my secretary, let's call her Gladys, and I said Gladys why don't you pull my trousers down. And Gladys thought for a moment and then she just smiled at me and said ...

JACK nods to MARY, prompting her response.

MARY. People want profit.
People want growth.
People want a return for their shareholders.
People want to do their own thing.
People want automatic gates.
People want matching accessories.
People want off-road vehicles.
People want weekends in Hong Kong.
People want vintage wines.
People want taste plus convenience.
People want neo-Georgian homes.
People want their kids at an all-white school.

JACK. Isn't that just amazing?
How could Gladys be so utterly stupid?
That's not what people want.
That's not what people want.
So I turned to Gladys and said ...
JACK nods at MARY once more.

MARY. People want to work in a mobile library.
People want to grow their own potatoes.

People want to sing in a male-voice choir.
People want to gather in a public place.
People want to live in the now.
People want to show their children right from wrong.
People want visionary leadership.
People want to know who's responsible.
People want to ensure this terrible tragedy never ever happens again.
People want a good night's sleep.
People want cash not cheques.
People want to forget the past.
People want a quiet life.
People want to pay less tax.
People want taste plus convenience.
People want neo-Georgian homes.
People want their kids at an all-white school.

JACK. And I turned to, Gladys, and I looked her straight in the eye and I said: That is what people want. *[regret/lust]* Gladys, Gladys. So, like mother.

JILL. Well, there you have it!

JACK. Please ...

JILL. In a nutshell!

JACK. *[to Jill]* This is not ... *[the time].*

JILL. Big man, talk the talk.

JACK. I was a good husband.

JILL. But he no walk the walk.

JACK. The commute was a nightmare!

JILL. A woman has needs!

JACK. I had sales targets!

JILL. I had to advertise in the local paper!

JACK. *[pleading]* These are business people.

JILL. I got sex in the small ads.

JACK. Business people ... you ... slut!

JILL. I am not a slut!

JACK. Pah!

JILL. I'm PROMISCUOUS ... there's a big difference!

A few moments of awkward silence. JACK returns to his presentation.

JACK. Thank you.
This is fantastic.
A room.
Full of rage and bitterness and insecurity and shame.

I feel humiliated.
You feel embarrassed.
The room is full of ... EMOTION.
And do you know what?
EMOTION ... is the NUMBER ONE tool for SUCCESS in business today.
We need to show more emotion, not less!
Cry, laugh, shout, fuck, kill!
LET ME HEAR YOU ROAR!
RAAARRRHHHH!!!
COME ON!
ROAR!
RAAARRRRHHH!!!

Let it all go!
That's it!
Emotion makes the world go round!
DON'T THINK.
FEEL.
It's that simple.
It's amazing isn't it?
It's not what you think, it's what you feel.
That's reality, that's business.

Let me just for moment tell you a story ... The other day I was on my way home, stuck in a lift, the most crowded lift you can imagine and I just turned to my P.A. Let's call her Kathy, and I said Kathy why don't you pull my trousers down. And Kathy smiled at me and said ...

JACK nods to prompt MARY.

MARY. Business is about money.
Business is about logic.
Business is about bottom line.
Business is about manageable risk.
Business is about facts.
Business is about cash flow.
Business is about cold hard numbers.

JACK. What a load of bull crap!
Have you ever heard anything so ...?
So I turned to Kathy, I looked her in the eye and said ...

MARY. Business is about feelings.
Business is about flowers and chocolate.
Business is about falling head over heels.
Business is about listening.
Business is about caring.
Business is about holding hands in the rain.
Business is about sneaking a look in the men's showers.
Business is about NOT being able to wait until your wedding night.
Business is about love.

JACK. And I looked at Kathy ...

JILL. *[laughing]* You are a joke!

JACK. *[emotional]* ... I looked at Kathy and I said: That's what business is about!
THAT'S WHAT BUSINESS IS ALL ABOUT, KATHY!

JILL. You haven't changed.

JACK. *[under his breath]* Slut.

JILL runs at JACK, grabbing his crotch.

JILL. Shut your scabby fucking cake-hole you impotent fucking liar!

MARY. Please!
Mind the gap!

Children can be such ...
Row, row, row your boat *gently* down the stream.

JILL. The limp get limper, the hard get harder, thus has it ever been!

JACK. I am not impotent!
I'm a businessman!

JACK is upset, runs to MARY.
She comforts him, strokes his hair maybe.

MARY. You remind me of a little boy who used to play in our garden. He wore green socks and a colander for a hat. And in his hand was a toy cap-gun. But the caps were damp and did not make a sound. And round and round the garden, flowerbeds smiled with lobelia and marigolds. Until one day the terrier next door would not stop barking and the little boy threw rocks at him until he bled and whimpered and died a death ...

JACK. *[to MARY]* Mother?

MARY. Moving on ...

JACK. Am I dreaming ...?

MARY. Our next speaker ...

JACK. Is there a God?

MARY. What can we say ...?

JACK. I can't believe it.

MARY. Is a bell necessary on a bike?

JACK. I'd recognize those shoes anywhere, mother!

JACK embraces MARY, burying his head in her bosom, inhaling her perfume.

MARY. *[pushing him away]* Get it off my chest!

JACK. I need you ... Mother, I'm lost.

MARY. Look I ... I'm a virgin! OK?

JACK. I don't care what you have or haven't done.

MARY. YOU'VE BEEN UNDER MY FEET ALL DAY! Just go! *JACK retreats. MARY composes herself.*
Yes. Thank you. Food for thought. We are painfully aware.
Certainly, it's a huge grey matter. We've raised a family of thorny issues. Some big questions that have really fallen down the back of the sofa in recent years. ... Does he who pays the piper, call his mother once a week? ... When the mice are away, does the cat play with himself?

JACK. *[to audience]* WHO KNOWS?
Who really knows?
Nobody.
And that's why ...
MAKE-BELIEVE is the NUMBER ONE tool for SUCCESS in business today.

JILL. You're making this up!

JACK. That's BUSINESS.
Make something up, then RUN with it!
Run for your life.
That my friends, is business!

JILL. Look, bottom line.
You're a basket case.
You have no equity.

JACK. Make-believe is money in the bank!
Invent your own world or someone else will do it for you!

JILL. I hate to break your crayons but this is bull crap ...

JACK. Business is about fantasy.

JILL. ...The fundamentals are weak as a kitten!

JACK. It's about smoke and mirror-balls ...
It's about pulling rabbits from a hole in the wall.
It's about wet dreams over Wendy in number 9.
It's about three-card tricks ...

JILL. This is a fucking dog and pony show!

JACK. ... It's about cartoon chicken mirages!
It's about the body and blood of Elvis Presley!

It's about wizards and witches and goblins and elves!
It's about chitty chitty bang bang ...!

MARY. That's enough!
Go to your room!
NOW!!

JACK exits, tail between legs.

MARY hesitates, then storms out after JACK.

JILL. *[calm, quiet]* Simple Minds are a support act.
In hindsight, that is our fundamental truth.

JILL. You paid your cash to see Madonna, Dylan, The Stones.
Here I am.

Pause.

When I agreed to speak to you here today, I was doing my hair.
Most people would have said no.
Most people would have said: I'm doing my hair ... No.
The fact that I'm here at all speaks volumes.
It speaks ...
It means ...
I think you know what it means.
Bad hair needs product, like a desert needs the rain.
Wrong.
Wrong.
Wrong.
You are stuck in the past.
You are thinking straight when you should be bent over backwards.
You are the square root of the problem.
So what I want you to do for me now is: Wipe the blackboard.

Mimes wiping a blackboard.

Wipe, wipe, wipe, wipe ...
Harder!
Wipe the blackboard!
Harder!
HARDER!
Good.
You have wiped out your long division, your past conditional, your irregular verbs.

You are clean.
From this moment on your life will never be the same.

JILL starts to move about the room.

Hi there, I'm the world's leading business mind.
I am the world's only business mind.
I know business.
I am business.
I am wanted in 547 countries.
I invented fire, the wheel, and the internet and who gets all the credit?
Bill fucking Gates.
The man is a flea.
He's a flea who needs to join a flea fucking circus.
This is a fact.
The Pope and the Dalai Lama, I buy and sell them for chips.
They are schoolboys with damp patches on the crotch of their schoolboy shorts.
Just like all the rest, they are unbelievable.
They are peddlers of piffle and bunkum.
If they knew business like I knew business.
That's why nine out of ten top chief executives wear my after-shave.
They smell.
They smell.
Because smell is the only truth.
Smell is a truth we can believe in.
Inhale.
Breathe it in.
Smell my truth.

JILL closes her eyes breathing in deeply through her nose

Can you smell it?
That is the future.
It stands to attention.
It's science fact.
SMELL TRAVELS FASTER THAN LIGHT.
That old chesnut.
You are smelling things that haven't even happened yet.
You don't believe me?
Your funeral.
And that is the trouble with nine out of ten chief executives!

Holding their noses when they should be sniffing at lampposts!
They should be breathing in the future.
Come on.
Smell it with me.
Sniff it up.
The future.

Pause.

In the future the world will walk with a crooked gait.
In the future everything we know will be chopped up and burnt on winter nights.
In the future mankind will amount to no more than the sum of its number.
In the future life will be uncannily sweet, yet sour.

JACK. In the future cars will run on sentimentality.
In the future air travel will be the stuff of science fiction.
In the future we will worship grandfather clocks.
In the future buses will all come along at the same time.

MARY. In the future daughters will become their fathers.
In the future mothers will become their daughters.
In the future sons will lay bare their inner-lives to strangers.
In the future fathers will hide their knitting behind the fashion page.

JILL. In the future our heads will be mobile phones.

MARY. In the future robots ...

JACK AND JILL. ... Will become our closest friends.

JACK. In the future ...

JILL. ... All photocopiers will be hunted down and destroyed.

MARY. In the future the internet will die ...

JACK, JILL, MARY. ... Unloved and alone, in a bed-sit.

JACK. In the future we'll castrate celebrities ...

MARY AND JILL. ... Celebrate sex offenders.

MARY. In the future travellers ...

JACK. ... Will be upgraded ...

JACK AND JILL. ... To business class.

JILL. In the future ...

MARY. ... Our prisons will be filled with pensioners.

JACK AND JILL. In the future ...

MARY. Shop-fitters will be prosecuted.

JACK. In the future skeletons will come out of the closet.

MARY. In the future the army will be gay.

JILL. In the future the air force will be straight.

JACK, JILL, MARY. In the future the navy will be wavy.

JILL. In the future they'll find a cure for kindness.
In the future ...

JILL AND MARY. ... We'll embrace sorrow like a long lost friend.

MARY. In the future we'll take hate class ...

JACK AND JILL. ... Straight after work.

JACK. In the future happiness will be the world's biggest killer ...

JILL AND MARY. ... After cancer.

MARY. In the future all the profits will be ploughed back into the community.

JILL. In the future the community ...

MARY AND JILL. ... Will spend the profits on cake.

JACK. In the future cake will be the key ...

MARY AND JILL. ... To your calorie-controlled diet.
In the future the chronically obese will compete for prizes.

JACK. In the future one Hoover bag will fit all.

JILL AND MARY. In the future delicious gourmet dinners will be ready in days.

JACK. In the future someone else will mess up your love life ...

JILL AND MARY. ... So you don't have to.

JILL. In the future the entire fabric of society will collapse ...

JACK AND MARY. ... And fit neatly in the boot of your car.

JACK. In the future ...

JILL. ... The sun will shine all day ...

MARY. ... And all of the night.
In the future palm trees will sprout from the cracks in every pavement.

JACK. In the future ...

JILL. ... Sharks will cruise down Main Street.
In the future ...

MARY AND JACK. ... The lark will lay down with the dodo.

JILL. *[whispered]* In the future.

JACK. *[whispered]* In the future.

MARY. *[whispered]* In the future.

MARY. In the future parents will be sent to bed without their tea.

JILL. In the future children will get drunk and fight over money.

JACK. In the future little girls will pick up strange men in parks.

JILL. In the future world power will rest in the hands of a tiny child ...

MARY. ... Called Donal.

JILL. In the future, everything we take for granted today will be different.
Everything we know today will be utterly shop-soiled.
Everything we do today will be cancelled out, written off.
Our way of doing business, our technology, our society.
All will be utterly different.
Day will be night and night will be day.
Black will be white and white will be grey.

Even the memory of my glory, my achievements will in time be obliterated, forgotten, thrown down the drain – like so much piss in a bucket to those ... those future alien-fuckers.

Silence

MARY. Thank you both.
Just to paraglide through the key points.
You'll correct me if I crumple, I'm sure.
In essence ...
The daftest hour is just before the alarm ...
Do unto others, as you will get done ...
And birds of a feather shop together ...
I believe that's it.

JACK nods, JILL seems to disagree.

So.
A number of pressing questions arising.
Who, what, when, where, why and how?
And others of their ilk.
But before we do ...
I'd like to big you up.

MARY encourages modest applause.

You give us faith, hope and charity.
You inspire us to dance on hot coals.
You encourage us to shoot the bourgeoisie.
You remind us the bins go out on Thursday.
You ask not what our country can do for us.
You ask what we can do in the country.
But that's another day's work.

Now.

It's probably time we threw up on the floor for questions.
Or we can open our legs for independent observers?

SONNY stands up at the back. The roving microphone goes to him.

SONNY. You are frauds.
You are liars.
You are perverts.
You are cheats.

You are fare dodgers.
You are sociopaths.
You are TV executives.
You are serial philanderers.
You are the seedy underbelly of the karaoke scene.
You are sneering snobs of the nouveau riche.
You are holocaust deniers.
You are elderly phone sex operatives.
You are cardboard cutouts.
You are the villains of daytime wrestling.
You are shopping centre Santas.
You are recidivist panty thieves.
You are county councillors.

JILL. Sonny?

JACK. Sonny is that you?

JILL. Those shoes, I'd recognize them anywhere.

JACK. Yes. It's him!

JILL. You're back!

SONNY. I'm not your ... !

JILL. Don't say it! Don't ... Your father is upset. Your father misses you. After you left ... your father cried. Your father hoped more than anything that you would go into business. Your father worked so hard for you. And then you were gone. Your father was so lonely. He was so lonely that he began to think. Your father began to think that all this ... was just an old tin bucket, clanking and rattling outside the back door. And then your father thought some more and he began to think that the bucket and ... and the door and the kitchen sink were all just figments of ... And then he began to think some more and he thought to himself, in his heart of hearts, he thought: What if my son does not exist? What if I dreamt him up last night in bed? What if it was a dream? But it was so real. There were bright colours and real feelings and a light breeze. How could that be a dream?

JACK. I put it out of my head!

JILL. It's OK now.
He's here now.
Our sonny.

SONNY. Don't call me sonny!

JACK. Please!
Give us another chance.
Whatever it was, just ...

JILL. Come home.

SONNY. You're pathetic.

JILL. We did our best.

JACK. Do you have any idea?

JILL. Bringing a life into this world.

SONNY. I believed in you.

JILL. We're your parents.

JACK. Children ask so many questions.

JILL. We tucked you in, didn't we?

JACK. We told you bedtime stories.

SONNY. Exactly!

JACK. We told the truth.

SONNY. They were Lies!

JILL. You'd better watch your step.

SONNY. What about Cinderella? What about Rapunzel?!

JILL. Rapunzel had wonderfully thick hair, OK?!

JACK. Just like her mother.

JILL. Conditioner. Salon conditioner.

SONNY. Here we go.

JACK. Look. Children need stories and certainty.

JILL. Children need ... boundaries.

SONNY. It was so dark up there.

JACK. You were out of control.

SONNY. I was only a child.

JACK. Can we not go over this again?

SONNY. No let's. Come on. Why?

JILL. I refuse to discuss this ...

SONNY. Why did you do it?!

JILL. You refused to believe in Santa Claus!
Refused.

JACK. Point blank.

SONNY. Because he doesn't exist.

JILL. He's Scandinavian. Of course he exists!

SONNY. I was frightened.

JACK. It was for your own good, to protect you.

JILL. It was business.

SONNY. Business?! What the hell is business? Haw?

JACK. Business is a strict code of practice.

JILL. Business gives us hope in times of recession.

JACK. Business forgives us our third quarter losses.

JILL. Business delivers us from muddled thinking.

JACK. Business clarifies our unique selling point.

JILL. Business justifies the cruelty we do unto others.

JACK. Business is what we believe in.

SONNY. But I don't believe in business.
I don't believe in global warming.
I don't even believe in romance.

JILL. No!

JACK. Your mother is upset.

SONNY. Look ... It's impossible to believe anything nowadays.

The more you know, the less ... You know?
I'm not an idiot.
I'm not short of a picnic or a full shilling.
I'm not witless, bird-brained, batty, touched, dim, dopey, nuts.
I just can't believe ... stuff.

JACK. Look it's not your fault. We never sat you down and ...

JILL. Tell him now.

SONNY. It's too late!

JILL. Tell him!

SONNY. *[hands over ears]* I'm not listening ... J'écoute pas! No te oigo! Ich kann Sie nicht hören!

JACK. Son, when a mummy and a daddy love each other very much, the daddy puts his little thing in mummy's ...

SONNY. *[covering his ears, singing to German anthem tune]* Eiscreme, Eiscreme über alles ...

JILL. Listen to your father when he's talking to you!

SONNY. Eiscreme, Eiscreme über alles ...

JILL. Look, you're adopted.
You were raised by wolves.
Aunt Peggy's your half-sister.

SONNY. What am I doing here? This was a big mistake.

SONNY goes for the door.

JACK. This is the real world Sonny.

JILL. *[stern]* Look, the reality is we are a small open economy on the edge of a forest ... No, not that. We are a small open economy beside a lake. The property has use of a boathouse, but one of the oars is missing and the other is on annual leave. Please ensure the farm gate is secured nightly as caribou will eat carrots.

JACK. Get it?!

SONNY. This is bull crap.

JILL. What did you just say?

SONNY. I said what a load of Bull Crap!

JACK. LANGUAGE! Please! *[to himself]* Fuck!

JILL. He was always a stubborn little ...

JACK. ... little cunt.

JILL. ... Yes. A little cunt.

MARY. Can I just remind you there are young children ... riding round without helmets.

JACK. Yes, yes. I'm sorry.
It's just he's come here and he's ...

JILL. This is a business seminar, Sonny.

SONNY. Yeah?
Well BUSINESS IS NONSENSE.
That's the sum.
That's the tower of Pisa.
Listen to yourselves.

You know nothing.
No one knows anything.
That's business.
It's a con.
It's cooked up.
It's hot air.
But you call it pre-heated oxygen.

JILL. Are you quite finished?

SONNY. I'll go now.

JILL. Great.

SONNY. I'm going.

JILL. Go.

Sonny exits the room.

JACK. Thank you!
Bon Voyage!
Well, it just shows you ...

JILL. Modern consumers are nuts.

SONNY bursts back in.

JACK. Yes?

SONNY. I'm not finished.

JACK. Bravo!

JILL. Share it with the class!

JACK. Why not?

JACK gestures to SONNY to come to the front.

SONNY. ... A long, long time ago.
On the television.
They found scrolls in a cave in the desert.
And the scrolls said: Turn Back.
There's nothing to see here.
It's a desert.
We've had nothing to drink for days.
We're going out now.
We may be some time.
Tell my wife I love her very much.
No full stop.
Just blank pages.
How do you think I felt?
Blank pages.
I couldn't take it.
Everything collapsed.
I had to end it all.

I ran out of the house and I kicked the old tin bucket outside the back door. Then I hopped the back wall and went down to the railway bridge. I stood on the parapet and I waited. Of course the 16.52 never came. So what do you do? What? You jump. But even gravity doesn't want you. What goes up, stays up. You float above the town with the railway bridge. You see the street sprawl, the weedy patios, the shopping centres, the church, children stoning rats behind the filling station. Up, up and cheap radio, jack hammers, tied-up Alsatians become a whisper, then the smell of fresh paint and slurry faint away. And now you're moving faster. You can see the sea from here and the mountains and countries and continents and clouds below and the shining curve of the earth against the curtain of outer space. And you're really shifting now. Leaving home at the speed of light. Now past the Moon, then Mars, Jupiter, Saturn, Uranus, Neptune, and little Pluto. Now the planets fade behind you and you're so, so far from home. And you're the smallest speck in the biggest emptiness ever dreamt of. For five years you hurtle at the speed of light through the vacuum dark until at last you meet your next-door neighbour – a burning yellow sun just like your own. But it doesn't end there, you keep going. Further and further away from a town with a railway bridge and a train that never came. You keep going, further then furthermore. At the speed of light. Now you are one hundred thousand light years from home. And now you see it. All this space, all these grains upon grains of light are a galaxy. The Milky Way opens her arms, herding four hundred billion stars in a silver swirl. You cry at the lonely beauty of it. It is too big to understand. But you can't stop. You must keep going. At the speed of light. Three billion light years pass you by and still you bolt further and further away from a town with a railway bridge and a train that never came. And now you look back, and each speck of light you see splashed across that everlasting cinescope is not a star. It is an entire galaxy. And it is impossible. It is incomprehensible ... It makes every atom of your body scream and just when you think you can't take it any more ... KKAA-LLLANG!! A cartoon collision with the very edge of the universe ... You have hit a giant wall made of tin ... And you look up ... And you realize that your universe, your everything, your vast entirety lives in the bottom of an empty old tin bucket outside the back door of some house in some town with a railway bridge and a train that never came.

Pause

MARY. *[pushing SONNY towards the exit]* Yes, look at the time.
Running out the door.
Where did it go?
Down the mountainside and out, out, out across the tundra.
Time within me, Time behind me, Time before me, Time beside me.
And who's going to clean up the mess?
I know, I know.
It's unreliable, like a stopped watch.
Won't budge an inch.
No home to go to.
It's made up.
Good for trains and boats and planes.
It lets off puffs of steam that we can't catch.
We can't untangle.

Like a ball of Nana's knitting wool, where's the start and where's the end?
Is there time for tea?
Maybe that's one for another day.
But most importantly.
Let's keep moving.
Let's not get ahead of ourselves.
We are where we are, aren't we?
We only have the room for a limited time.
How does one respond to that?
How?

JACK takes the floor.

JACK. Ha, ha, ha, ha, ha, HA!
That's my boy!
I love it, I love it, I love it.
Well done you little ...
Look, we understand.
The way you're feeling.
Sometimes you lose your way.
Because it's hard and ...
It's leafy.
It's sweaty.
It's full of wild animals and ...
You've got cannibals.
You've got cheetah.
You've got boy.
You've got Tarzan.
Business is a jungle.
Yes.
We know that.
But don't give up.
Never give up.
Chop those trees down.
See the wood.
Believe.

Hey, let me just for a moment tell you a story. A long time ago, before you were born, I was involved in the footwear business. Once upon a time, my creditors were closing in, the banks were threatening to foreclose, my staff were on strike and all I had was a factory and one last piece of leather to make one last pair of shoes. So, I laid out the piece of leather in the middle of the factory floor thinking – tomorrow I will cobble together one last pair of shoes and call it a day. So I went to bed with a heavy heart, convinced I was a failure. But when I opened up the factory the next day what did I see? Not the leather, but a pair of exclusive hand-made designer shoes. I couldn't believe it. In fact, they were so to-die-for that the liquidator bought them on the spot for cash and offered to invest in the company. I was over the moon. Now I had enough money to buy leather for two pairs of shoes. And believe it or not, the next morning it was the same story – this time there were two pairs of exclusive hand-made designer shoes in the middle of the factory floor. Unbelievable. Suddenly, the business was really picking up, soon I had paid off my debts and my cash flow problems were a distant memory. But one question was bothering me. Who was making those exclusive hand-made designer shoes? One night I decided to find out. I hid myself behind a pile of cardboard boxes and waited ... and waited. Just after midnight, an extraordinary thing happened. A group of tiny elves, as naked as the day they were born, climbed through the window and set about making exclusive hand-made designer shoes from the leather I'd left out. I couldn't believe my eyes. The elves had just finished the job and were about to leave when I revealed myself. 'Guys!' I said, 'How can I ever thank you?' And do you know what they said? All those elves wanted was a little elf suit each. They were so poor they couldn't even afford clothes. So I said you can have clothes and you can stay with me here in my factory. Everyone's a winner. So, the elves moved in, production increased and sales were booming. But do you know what? Next thing there's complaints from the elves. I give them clothes, I give them a roof over their head but now they're looking for three meals a day and reasonable working hours. (18 hours a day, I think that's reasonable.) Anyway, industrial relations got so bad that I had no option. I went straight down to World of Toys and sourced a batch of miniature manacles. 'This hurts me more than it hurts you', I told them, as I chained them to their tiny workstations. But would you believe what they do next? One by one, the vindictive little bastards go and die on me. Next thing I can't fill orders, the bank won't give me credit and the business goes to the wall.

I am left with nothing.
All thanks to a bunch of elves.
Unbelievable, isn't it?
But do you think I quit?
Do you think I gave up on business?
Hell no.

Look at me!
I am where I am today!
Right here!

JILL. Now do you see?
Virtualization is the key to existence in times of market volatility.

SONNY. Que?

JILL. Do you want to end up sweeping the streets?
Do you want to end up a bin man or a teacher!

SONNY. No entiendo nada.

JILL. Have you even thought about pension provision?
What happens to your lifestyle after you're gone?
People like a big funeral nowadays.
Thought about that?
Well?
Answer me!

SONNY. *[circus ringmaster]*
Meine damen und herren! [ladies and gentleman]
Congratulazioni tutti! [congratulations everybody]
Hajimemashite! [nice to meet you]
Boa vinda! [welcome]
Bu son derece tehlikelidir. [this is extremely dangerous (in Turkish)]
Du måste koncentrera sig hela tiden. [you must concentrate at all times (in Swedish)]
Luga moja haitoshi. [one language is never enough (in Swahili)]
And so, I give you ...
Palabras! [words]
Palabras, palabras....!

SONNY encourages applause

JILL. You've got to stop!

SONNY. ... Palabras, palabras, palabras, palabras ...!

JILL. You're sticking your head in the sand!

SONNY puts on a paper bag mask.

JILL gets upset and has to leave the room for a moment.

JACK. It's just a phase.

JILL. I'm at my wits end!

JACK. *[comforting]* It's just a phase.

Pause

JILL. You're right.
It all makes sense.
Everything makes perfect sense.
He's wilful, recalcitrant, contumacious.
Just like me, when I was a little girl.

JACK. Yes.

JILL. When you think about ...

JACK. Yes.

JILL. The things I got up to.

JACK. Yes.

JILL. It reminds me of when I was a little girl. So, I'm living in a little cottage in a village at the edge of a big deep dark forest and one day my mother asks me to bring some cake and a pot of honey to my grandmother, to my grandmother who lives on the other side of the forest, the big deep dark forest. Don't dilly dally, don't delay, don't talk to strangers, don't stray off the path, don't pick flowers, don't pick your nose and stand up straight while I'm talking to you, says my mother, slapping me across the face. But of course, I'm halfway through the forest when I find a beautiful glade full of flowers. And of course, I stop and I pick the flowers. And next thing I hear this growling voice behind me. It's a stranger, who sounds just like some sort of wolf. And the wolf tells me I'm a very good girl and a very pretty girl. And the wolf asks me where I'm going. And I tell the wolf about my mother and how she warns me not to speak to strangers. And the wolf says he understands me. He really understands. When I finally get to the other side of the big deep dark forest, grandmother's front door is half open and it all seems very quiet. I really should be guessing everything's not quite right when I see blood on the floor. But I'm a little girl, what do I know? Really, it's not until grandmother gets all defensive about the size of her eyes and her ears, that I start to get nervous. And next thing I know the wolf is eating me alive, there's blood everywhere and I'm screaming like fuck. But it's no good, he swallows me and my little basket in three gulps. And so there I am in this wolf's stomach, dying a death. But suddenly there's a knock at the door. And it's the woodcutter. 'Everything all right grandmother, I heard a commotion', he says. 'Not a bother', says the wolf in a deep growl of a voice. But now I'm screaming and screaming from inside the wolf, louder than I've ever screamed before. 'Is that a little girl in your stomach grandmother', asks the woodcutter. 'It's a family matter!' growls the wolf. 'But grandmother, isn't there some sort of law?' asks the woodcutter. 'She's been a very naughty girl!' shouts the wolf-granny. 'Fair enough. Sorry for disturbing you,' says the woodcutter. And off he goes. Can you believe it?

Carrying her microphone, JILL goes to SONNY.

I had a sharp little pair of pinking shears in my basket.
[emotional again] And I am where I am today.
I'll tell you one thing.
I learnt my lesson that day.
I learnt my lesson and I never forgot it.
Do you hear me?
Are you going to say anything?

SONNY faces JILL still wearing his paper bag mask. He grabs JILL's microphone. SONNY raises the microphone to his mouth, or rather to his paper bag. We hear a garbled nonsense poem (possibly 'Dyr Bul Shchyl' by Aleksei Kruchenykh) and SONNY mimes to the cadence of the sounds as if he's making a rousing speech to the audience.

JILL and JACK become agitated.

JACK. What can you do ...?

JILL. What can you say ...?

JACK. This isn't business!

JILL. In the future, there will be a law.

JACK. Business is about control and command.

JACK and JILL try to push SONNY out the door.

SONNY keeps coming back.

MARY. At this point.
Can we ...?

JILL. In the future, your neighbours will be cold war spies.

MARY. Perhaps we could ...?

JACK. Business is about moving the goalposts.

JILL. In the future, we'll carry a bigger stick.

MARY. Points of view are incredible from tall buildings.
We accept that ...

JACK. Business is about a really aggressive campaign.

JILL. In the future, we'll medicate the unconvinced.

JACK. Business is about 'my name here and here and here.'

MARY. There's a dizzying array ...
Vertigo's super flick ...

JILL. In the future, your books will keep us warm at night.

SONNY bursts into the room once more. This time he's joined by the sound of a blaring Balkan brass band. SONNY dances wildly at Jack and Jill.

MARY. Yes, rope gets frayed around the edges!
It's the work of friction!

JACK. Business is about my country right or wrong.

JACK and JILL push SONNY out once more. Elevator music replaces the brass band.

JILL. In the future, blacks and coloureds will have private beaches.

MARY. The days are getting short.
And there's precious little light.

SONNY comes back again, bringing the brass band music with him. Once more he is ejected and the elevator music resumes.

JACK. Business is about living room.

JILL. In the future, you'll be judged by the shape of your skull.

SONNY bursts back in. JACK and JILL try to cut the Balkan music but it won't stop.

MARY. Life's a bitch!
Life's a bitch on a beach with a better tan than you.
I hope she fries in olive oil.

They chase SONNY around the room.

JACK. Business is about jewels in the jungle.

MARY. Don't drink the water!

JILL. In the future, you'll hide your face in public.

SONNY causes havoc, knocking over the furniture and throwing papers in the air.

MARY. Legionnaires, I told them!

JACK. Business is about slicing up your children's private parts.

MARY. You'll be decimated.

They grab Sonny, but he escapes again.

JILL. In the future, we'll drown you till you talk.

MARY. You'll spend the trip with trousers round your ankles.

JACK. Business is about planting bombs in Pizza Hut.

JILL. In the future, cattle trains will take you on holidays.

MARY. Is that what you want?!

JACK. Business is about 'You're terrorists! We're freedom fighters'.

MARY. Some sort of consolation?

JILL. In the future, you will not ask questions.

MARY. A car? A caravan?

JACK. Business is about shock and awe.

MARY. A week in Raffles, Singapore?

JILL. In the future, traitors will be shot on sight.

JACK. Business is about the sweet smell of napalm in the morning.

JILL. In the future, your sons will disappear overnight.

Jack and Jill grab SONNY again. He struggles hard.

JACK. Business is about the only good Indian's a dead Indian.

JILL. In the future, we'll rape your father, your daughter and your son.

JACK. Business is about the Tutsis, Abos, Armenians, Orphans, Academics, Cripples, Gypsies, Jews, Lefty Types and you.

JACK and JILL drag SONNY towards the exit, kicking and screaming.

JILL. In the future, we'll truck them all to a stadium on the outskirts of town and let them have it!

MARY grabs a basket full of individually wrapped biscuits and walks about throwing them to the audience.

MARY. Tea, coffee, snacks?!
Tea, coffee, snacks?!
Tea, coffee, snacks ...?! *[continues over the following]*

JACK. Business is about NEVER EVER having to say you're sorry!

JILL. In the future, we won't be joking we'll be deadly fucking serious!

JACK and JILL exit, dragging the struggling SONNY with them.

JACK. *[from off]* Why don't you pull my trousers down!?
Why don't you PULL MY TROUSERS DOWN?!

MARY. BECAUSE THEY'RE INDIVIDUALLY WRAPPED FOR FRESHNESS AND CONVENIENCE!

Pause

Any questions?

Long Pause.

The mayhem is over. The actors are quite calm and 'normal' now. The other actors agree, they hold up photographs of themselves – genuine personal mementos. They each tell a personal story related to the photograph. Each story starts with 'This is me ... ' Their stories speak of life, family, love, death. They are true stories.

When all four stories have been told, the song 'It Won't Be Very Long' by Sam Cooke and The Soul Stirrers plays and the light fades as the actors look around, connecting with each other and the audience.

END.

SWAMPOODLE

Author's note

Swampoodle was written for performance in the Uline Arena – a semi-derelict 9,000-seater indoor sports arena in Washington DC. The space is currently used as a car park. The Uline is located next to Union Station in what was the city's historic Swampoodle area – an Irish-American shantytown.

Swampoodle premiered at The Uline Arena, Washington D.C. in May 2011.

Original Cast

Clare Barrett
Rachel Beauregard
Michael John Casey
Chris Dinolfo
Judith Ingber
Maya Jackson
Jason McCool
Adrienne Nelson
Karl Quinn
Rosemary Regan
Stephanie Roswell
Anastasia Wilson

Director: Jo Mangan
Production Designer: Ciaran Bagnall
Lighting Designer: Marianne Meadows
Costume Designer: Niamh Lunny

The audience enters the half-dark Uline Arena. At the far end of the arena, MJ is sweeping. His back to us. Raising dust. The rumble of trains passing, their bells chiming. MJ turns and sees the audience.

MJ. Hey!
You.
People.
Yes.
You.
Come here.
What do you think you're doing?
Here.
A rundown part of town.
At night.
In a parking lot?
Are you out of your ...
Look at this place.

He looks around.

Don't look at me, I only work here but ...
What were you thinking?
People end up dead.
Sure.
Your funeral but ...
Listen, we're here now.
Listen, might as well make the ...
Listen.

He listens.

That's Tiber Creek.
Under your feet.
You heard me.
Tiber Creek.
Down deep.
He don't say a whole bunch.
He just keeps rolling along.
No Mississippi, nah.
Just a muddy stream.
Running through here.
Through Swampoodle.

He raises the dust with his brush.

Swampoodle.

They built it up.
They knocked it down.
And now ...

He grabs the dust cloud, then shows us his open hand.

All human life is here.
But Tiber Creek ...
Just sayin'.
Life ain't gonna live itself, now is it?

MJ reflects, then a thought comes to him.

This is where John Lennon sang I want to hold your hand.
And they screamed and screamed and screamed.
It was a wonderful show.

He indicates the whole space.

Go on.
It's all yours.
Nobody's stopping you.
Go.

MJ exits.

The audience are left alone in the dark of the space. In the distance, Rudolf Nureyev prepares. He powders his face. Far off we hear a man sing the Irish melody 'Trotting to the Fair'. Nureyev assumes a ballet pose. But as he does so he begings coughing uncontrollably, and the light fades to black.

From another part of the darkened arena, Adrienne and Clare enter.

ADRIENNE. *[nervous, in the dark]* Hello?! Who's there?!

A light goes on illuminating the audience.

What are you doing here?

CLARE. *[prompting]* Who's here for Swampoodle?

ADRIENNE. Who's here for Swampoodle?!

CLARE. *[prompting]* Hands up ...

ADRIENNE. Hands up ... All those for Swampoodle over here. Thank you.

CLARE. *[whispers to Adrienne]* The show is over.

ADRIENNE. I know that. They don't know. I do know.

CLARE. Aren't you going to ...?

ADRIENNE. Ladies and gentlemen. You're here now. So, I think you all should know that the show ...

CLARE. *[quietly]* ... over.

ADRIENNE. The show is wonderful! Yes ... Look, the show is over. OK? We have just done the show.

CLARE. What's done is done.

ADRIENNE. Yes but ...

CLARE. Life is short?

ADRIENNE. Can we ...?

CLARE. Move on?

ADRIENNE. Yes.

CLARE. *[reads from clipboard]* When entering the parking lot, please drive in the present with one eye on the road and one eye in the rear view mirror as ...

ADRIENNE. Clare ...

CLARE. ... large objects may appear trivial in hindsight.

ADRIENNE. Thank you, Clare! *[off-mic]* Tell the guys, they're here to see the fucking show.

CLARE. Sorry?

ADRIENNE. Go and tell them. They're here to see the fucking show.

Clare goes hesitantly.

CLARE. *[calls out]* They're here for the 'fucking-show'!

ADRIENNE. No! No ...! The supporting cast. Go!

Clare runs off to find the others.

Awkward pause.

I understand. It was 8.30. Yes. Originally. It was originally advertised for 8.30. But some of our leads got parts. In Showboat. And of course, they had evening shows so we ... I didn't want a part in Showboat if you're committed to a show you stick with it you don't go changing the schedule, you don't go changing the performance times to suit the lead actors, I mean I'm a lead actor ... an off-lead and Katy's still here, she's a lead actor, she didn't want a part in Showboat, she is committed, Katy and I have a lovely scene, we can do it, we can do all sorts of scenes for you without those lead actors off rehearsing Showboat ... *[awkard pause]* Mercy. Time goes by, doesn't it? When it's just you, with a whole bunch of time, and space. I feel like an ant. A little she-ant just waiting for something to ... *[runs off]* Katy! Katy?!

Adrienne exits.

Clare enters.

CLARE. Adrienne?

Clare sees the audience.

Oh ... we ... yes ... any minute ...

MJ appears.

MJ. *[at Clare]* This is where Nureyev danced on a hot summer night.
And the ladies came to watch in furs.
It was a wonderful show.

CLARE. Yes, right ... perhaps ... *[reads]* 'The Uline – A short history'. Built in 1941 by Miguel Uline, the Uline Ice Arena has played many parts. In the early days, it hosted sporting events from hockey to boxing to Midget Car Racing. The Uline was also the home of family entertainment in DC, hosting Bailey and Barnum circus, Roy Rogers' Rodeo, the Royal Ballet, the Ice-Capades, the Uline Water Follies and Roller-Skate Derbies, to name but a few. The arena is best known for hosting The Beatles first ever American concert in 1964 ...

She's still alone.

... Since then, the Uline has continued ...*[skimming through]* dum dee dum dee dum ... In May 1971, it was a temporary prison for anti-war protesters and other such peaceniks ... For a time the Uline was a church: The Miracle Faith Centre. Later, it was central to the city's hygiene program, serving as a trash transfer centre and today the Uline is vital to DC's transport network, recognized as one of the city's premier parking lots ...

Adrienne returns with Chris, Jason, Karl, Rachel, Stacy and Stephanie. They appear to be half-costumed and a little confused.

RACHEL. Hello.

STACY. Hi.

ADRIENNE. *[to Clare]* Where's Katy? Get Katy!

Clare goes looking for Katy.

CHRIS. Hello.

JASON. Hey.

Stephanie stays conspicuously in the background. Jason tweets and takes iphone photos throughout.

ADRIENNE. *[to the cast]* They're here for the show.

RACHEL. Oh, OK. For the show ...

ADRIENNE. The show goes on.

KARL. The show is over.

ADRIENNE. No. The show goes on.

RACHEL. What ...?

The cast take Adrienne aside to question her.

ADRIENNE. *[half-heard]* What do you mean ...? No I am not high. I'm not high.

MJ. *[indicating the exit]* If I were you I'd carpe diem, or somethin'.

Adrienne seems to have won the agreement of the cast.

ADRIENNE. I should point out, we are working with a skeleton cast ...

MJ. I see dead people ...

ADRIENNE. But since you are all here now, we've decided to present an unscheduled performance of our show, Swampoodle ... once we have our remaining lead actors.

MJ. Actor, singular.

Clare returns, whispers to Adrienne. In the distance, Katy walks to her car. Adrienne runs to her.

ADRIENNE. Katy! Katy sweetheart! They're here for the show.

In the distance, Katy and Adrienne have a heated debate.

RACHEL. Bear with us, guys.

CHRIS. We're going to do this show if it kills us.

MJ. They die on stage every night so ...

STACY. We're all very proud of Swampoodle.

MJ. There's no script.

Katy gets in her car and starts to drive out of the building.

KARL. It's a devised physical-slash-visual spectacle that explores the boundaries of what and how theatre can be.

MJ. There's no story.

CHRIS. There is too!

MJ. Seen it. No story.

Adrienne runs alongside the car, knocking on the driver's window. The car pulls away and exits.

ADRIENNE. OK, leave! Go ahead! By the way, I'm sleeping with your boyfriend, you piece of shit!

Adrienne continues to hurl abuse at the departing car.

MJ. The talent has left the building.

CHRIS. OK ...

STACY. We all feel very passionate about this project.

RACHEL. You've got to be passionate, right? Otherwise, what's the point?

Adrienne returns, distraught.

ADRIENNE. What's the point? Katy's gone.

CHRIS. Who needs Katy?!

RACHEL. We don't need her.

KARL. We all hate Katy.

STACY. *[taken aback]* Karl ...

KARL. We do.

STACY. I like her ...

CHRIS. Oh, please. Katy sucks.

ADRIENNE. I thought it was just me.

RACHEL. We love you, Adrienne. *[the audience]* We love Adrienne and we all hate Katy. That's number 1. And number 2, I think we owe it to all of you here who have waited so patiently and come to such a rundown part of town in the middle of the night, to do this show.

CHRIS. We're all part of this thing! Whoop!

Chris punches the air. Encourages audience applause.

Right here and now. Let's do it!

CLARE. *[reads]* You can catch Zara, Alan and Gregg in Show Boat at Arena Stage from June 30th. Tickets can be ...

ADRIENNE. Thank you Clare! Thank you! OK. Yes. We are here now. We don't have very long. We must make the most. The show goes on.

MJ. It'll run and run, believe me ...

MJ exits.

ADRIENNE. So here we are. Where to begin? The Uline Arena. As you may know, many great artists have performed here. Nureyev, Duke Ellington, Bob Dylan ...

CLARE. I already ...

ADRIENNE. And you mentioned The Beatles ... ?

The cast go crazy, Beatle-mania style, reaching out to touch the audience. 'I want to hold your hand' plays loud. The cast then run screaming into the darkness. Adrienne is left alone with the audience.

ADRIENNE. I do apologize. Our supporting cast are highly suggestible to ... 'the B word'. They all trained at the Pavlov school, so perhaps our rehearsal was a tad too intensive ... Clare!

Adrienne rushes off into the dark.

A moment, then we hear a trumpet play. Up on the balcony amid the battered bleachers, a trumpet player stands. He plays a slow lament, which we recognise as 'I want to hold your hand'. The light fades.

Adrienne has appeared in another part of the space. She beckons the audience. The audience moves to Adrienne and the cast gradually rejoin the group.

ADRIENNE. Hello? Hello?! Yes, I am sorry. Things happen, don't they? But we're all here now. So if you wouldn't mind ... We need to move on. But before we perform Swampoodle, I'm sure you would love to have our supporting cast introduce themselves and give a little background. So, who's first?

Stacy is first in the line. She's about to speak

STACY. OK ... I ...

CHRIS. Hi, I'm Chris. I'm an actor, with a lot of experience in theatre, film and TV. My other abilities include martial arts, horseback riding and sword-fighting and my playing age is 25 to 35 although I feel I could go as low as 19.

ADRIENNE. And Swampoodle ...?

CHRIS. What is Swampoodle? I guess it's a show, and I'm in it.

ADRIENNE. *[prompting]* What does it mean to you?

CHRIS. I'm sorry ...?

KARL. We are all very fond of Chris. He's not an intellectual.

CHRIS. Thank you.

ADRIENNE. What have you got to offer, Karl?

Karl ponders for a moment. Then with a flourish he recites – at first full of pomp, but gradually he begins to speak with simplicity and truthfulness.

KARL. All the world's a stage,
And all the men and women merely players:
They have their exits and their entrances;
And one man in his time plays many parts,
His acts being seven ages. At first the infant,
Mewling and puking in the nurse's arms.
And then the whining school-boy, with his satchel
And shining morning face, creeping like snail
Unwillingly to school. And then the lover,
Sighing like furnace, with a woeful ballad
Made to his mistress' eyebrow. Then a soldier,
Full of strange oaths and bearded like the pard,
Jealous in honour, sudden and quick in quarrel,
Seeking the bubble reputation.
Even in the cannon's mouth. And then the justice,
In fair round belly with good capon lined,
With eyes severe and beard of formal cut,
Full of wise saws and modern instances;
And so he plays his part.
The sixth age shifts
Into the lean and slipper'd pantaloon,
With spectacles on nose and pouch on side,
His youthful hose, well saved, a world too wide
For his shrunk shank; and his big manly voice,
Turning again toward childish treble, pipes
And whistles in his sound. Last scene of all,
That ends this strange eventful history,
Is second childishness and mere oblivion,
Sans teeth, sans eyes, sans taste, sans everything.

Woody Hermann's big band tune BLUE FLAME plays. The performers move through the space.

THE CAST. Patrick Ferban got full of Swampoodle whisky last night.
Ran amuck with a pistol, two knives and a shillailah.
Got in some houses on H Street and chased the people out.
And we dance.
A regular riot occurred on L street yesterday.
An Irish gang stole a keg of beer from Sullivan's saloon.
And drank it.
Got in a free fight. Took six police to quell it.
And we dance.
John Doran went home from work last night and found his wife Kate a raving maniac.
Opened his front door in Swampoodle.
And Mrs Doran tried to make him bald-headed.
With a kettle of boiling water.
Mrs Doran was discharged from St Elizabeth's Asylum but a short while ago.
On account of a similar eccentricity.
And we dance.
A Goat alley woman named Bessie Howard.
Better known as Sadie Gibson.
Charged with robbery from the person of Henry Jackson.
Sadie asked him for five cents one night down in Goat Alley.
I ain't got no five centses, he responded.
Sadie threw her arms about him.
Incidentally seizing his pocketbook, containing seven-eighty.
Two years in the penitentiary.
Set to screaming.
When they took her down.
And we dance.
Saturday night, a coloured man named Edward Cole had his skull fractured.
A blow on the side of the head.
Administered by an Italian, Vincent Bernadina.
In a row, in a bar, on G Street.
At 7.45 last evening, Cole died from the effects of his wound.
And we dance.

ADRIENNE. *[as if nothing's happened]* Thank you Karl. Moving on. When you are in a show like Swampoodle, I think it's really important that everyone gets a chance to share so I'll throw it open …

Stacy believes it's now her turn to speak but Adrienne doesn't notice.

Jason, would you like to say something.

Jason is tweeting on his iphone.

JASON. Say? What? Yes I do have something to say ... let me just tweet this and ... *[sends tweet]* Yes, I guess I have been doing a ton of thinking and blogging and tweeting about the process. I know some of you have been following McCool-in-Swampoodle-dot-blogspot-dot-com. For me, as an Irish person ...

KARL. He is not Irish.

JASON. For me, as an Irish person, I think it's amazing what the Irish people of Swampoodle achieved. It's incredible to think about how the Irish built Washington. They built the White House, they built the Capitol, they built the Lincoln Memorial, they built the railways, they built the streets, they built office blocks and they built all of the houses and of course they built this, the Uline. So I guess I'm thinking about all these Irish people who built this great city and how we've forgotten them.

Jason takes us to a spot in the centre of the Uline.

Also, like the biggest fight fan, so I'm thinking about all the great fighters who fought here in the Uline. OK, here's one that gets me every time. Right here on this spot in 1948, the great Rocky Marciano knocked out Gilbert Cardone in just thirty six seconds. His second fastest career K.O. Incredible. I mean, to me, Rocky was a real Irish hero.

CHRIS. What?! Rocky was Italian!

JASON. He was Irish, Dinolfo! He was Irish!

ADRIENNE. Let's not get totally hung up on the Irish. The show isn't all about Irish people. Big deal, they built a lot of stuff but ... A lot of my friends are Irish. But it's true what they say, isn't it?

JASON. Excuse me?

ADRIENNE. I'm going off point. What I'm trying to say Swampoodle is home to many different nationalities, races, religions. There are black people ...

MJ. There's one black person.

ADRIENNE. ... Historically, in Swampoodle. Swampoodle always had an African-American population. And of course, they suffered terrible prejudice. Even this building, the Uline was segregated during the 40's. But they fought it and they overcame it and since then, many many great African-American artists have performed here. On stage right over here.

JASON. Duke Ellington.

ADRIENNE. Yes.

RACHEL. Paul Robeson sang Ol' Man River here.

Stacy (an African-American woman) puts her hand up tentatively.

KARL. Ray Charles.

MJ. Chuck Brown ... Wonderful show.

ADRIENNE. Yes, yes ... what I'm trying to say is shouldn't they have a voice? Shouldn't they be allowed ... *[spotting Stacy's hand is up]* Stacy? Yes?

STACY. I just wanted to say that, to me Swampoodle is about the evolution of the space. It's about taking inspiration from the people who have passed in and out of it. So, it's not that the building itself has done something or that it is a monument but rather we are here to imagine the lives of the people who performed here, who came here, who lived their lives in this neighbourhood. Life hasn't changed. It's just different people in a different time. These stories are still happening. And Swampoodle, whatever it is, allows us to see life through a different lens. Because life being lived is as important as any one event in history.

ADRIENNE. OK ... That's certainly one way of looking at it. Anyone else? Stephanie?

STEPHANIE. *[nervous]* Me? Really? I'm terrible at this ...

STACY. *[encouraging]* Go on. It's OK.

STEPHANIE. I know, I know ... I'm an actor. But I just. Talking ... Not Acting ... Eek ... OK. Calm down Stephanie.

RACHEL. Go for it Stephanie.

STEPHANIE. OK. Where do I start? This place. I don't know. So many stories. I don't know, to me it's like a ghost story. Like, sometimes when I'm in here I get really ... Did you hear that?

RACHEL. What?

CHRIS. Stephanie ...?

STEPHANIE. A voice? Voices ...? No? OK ... OK, maybe just a garbage truck ... And breathe. Anyway, the story that got me most is the one all about the disappearance of Swampoodle. So right now, we're in what was Swampoodle, which was this truly notorious Irish ...

JASON. Notorious? I'm sorry?

STEPHANIE. Well, yeah, it was an Irish neighbourhood, and so you've got crime, drunkenness, prostitution ...

JASON. Whoa! The Irish built this city.

CHRIS. What are you talking about? The Italians built this city!

JASON. The Italians never did nothing, Dinolfo!

CHRIS. We built DC, McCool! We built it!

Jason and Chris square up.

The others try to separate them.

A scuffle ...

ADRIENNE. It's improvised, it's all improvised!

CHRIS. I will end you!

ADRIENNE. We're very passionate! And scene!

JASON. I will end you!

ADRIENNE. And scene!

The others separate Chris and Jason. There are two camps now.

And scene. So sorry. Moving on. Rachel?

STEPHANIE. Hey! I'm talking here! So, way back in the day, the Irish are living their lives back in Irish-land when out of the blue they're hit with this terrible drought ...

KARL. She means the Irish potato famine.

STEPHANIE. One million Irish people die in this terrible drought and one million people are forced to emigrate, to DC.

KARL. No, not exactly ...

STEPHANIE. Karl, we know you're trying to make a point with the hairstyle but this is hard for me, OK?

KARL. It was a famine and they did not all come ...

STEPHANIE. The point is life turns you inside out and upside down and next thing you know you're here.

Stephanie moves to a spot in the arena.

Right here, in Swampoodle. In Jackson Alley. You're here now. You survived.

During the following a sad clown enters and performs a number of daily domestic rituals in a makeshift living room area set up in a corner of the arena. She's joined by MJ.

You have to keep on living. Getting up in the morning. Going to work. Looking after your children. Feeding your animals. Meeting people you know in the street. Going to church. Eating and drinking. Because you never know ... And just when you think everything is ... You wake up one bright morning in 1907 and Swampoodle is completely gone. They've gone and built Union Station slap bang right on top of Swampoodle.

KARL. *[to audience]* Historically, that is wildly inaccurate ...

STEPHANIE. Look ginger nut, that's what happened! Somebody built a rail yard in a residential area. Somebody built a railway station on top of the Irish.

JASON. The Italians!

CHRIS. You're damn right we did!

JASON. The Italians killed Swampoodle!

CHRIS. And what you gonna do about it!?

A vaudville/circus style fight breaks out between two sides. The crashing, urgent music of scene 1, Swan Lake plays. A bulldozer enters and demolishes the living room area, crushing furniture and props. The bulldozer driver jumps from his cab and is chased into the dark by most of the cast. Only Clare and MJ remain amid the wreckage.

MJ. And the show goes on.

Clare picks up a chair leg, distraught.

CLARE. Jesus. What are we going to do?

MJ. A chair is a chair.

CLARE. It's not a chair, it's the entire set!

MJ. The show goes on.

CLARE. There's no bulldozer in the script!

MJ. This is where they bulldozed Jackson Alley.
And ran a railroad right through Swampoodle.
It was a wonderful show.

CLARE. What?

MJ. No curtain call.

CLARE. *[confused]* No curtain call?

MJ. It will run and run and run.

CLARE. What are we going to do?

MJ. Bulldozers never sleep.
Trains wait for no man.
Life's too short by half a yard.
Grab it while you can.

CLARE. What!?

MJ. Ah, just something I'm workin' on.

MJ exits, sweeping perhaps. The rest of the cast return.

ADRIENNE. I'm sorry. I do apologize. Clare, where do we start?

CLARE. Where? I don't know ... I ... The Nazis?

ADRIENNE. Of course. The Nazis meet Malcolm X. A wonderful scene.

Preparations for the scene begin in the background.The cast get into bathing suits. They spray water in the air with hosepipes. Ladies and gentlemen, this may take a little time to set up but it will be well worth the wait. Clare, would you like to put it in context for us?

CLARE. *[reads from clipboard]* This scene is our tribute to 1960's racial politics and the famous Uline Water Follies with their synchronized swimming delights ...

ADRIENNE Ladies and gentlemen, filling the pool may take a little longer than we have time here for.

CLARE. *[reads]* ... Let your imagination run wild as our heroes dive into a raging sea of mutual hatred ...

ADRIENNE. Thank you Clare. However did we block this?

CLARE. *[consulting the clipboard]* I ... OK ... I think ... The American Nazi storm troopers enter from over here? And paddle about in the shallow end. Nation of Islam dives in over there. Malcolm X swims over this direction and Nazi boss Rockwell treads water about here in the fascist lane ...

The cast practice a choreographed routine – synchronized swimming on dry land.

CLARE. Oh. Adrienne, we don't have Greg.

ADRIENNE. We don't have Greg?

CLARE. Showboat.

ADRIENNE. Showboat ... and he's such a wonderful Nazi. Karl would you mind standing in as Rockwell?

KARL. No.

ADRIENNE. Wonderful.

KARL. No I won't do it.

ADRIENNE. The show, Karl ...

KARL. Adrienne, the notion of playing an anti-Semitic demagogue, who peddled a philosophy of racial supremacy makes me extremely uncomfortable.

ADRIENNE. So you won't play Rockwell?

KARL. I can't play Rockwell, Adrienne. The very notion makes me sick.

ADRIENNE. OK then ...

KARL. Can I play Malcolm X?

ADRIENNE. You want to play Malcolm X.

KARL. He's a life-long hero of mine.

ADRIENNE. OK.

KARL. It's because I'm white, isn't it?

ADRIENNE. No! Gracious no! I just thought Stacy would be our Malcolm tonight.

KARL. She's a woman. She can't play Malcolm.

ADRIENNE. Karl, sexism has no place in this production.

Karl goes to get Stacy.

KARL. This is ridiculous. It's ... racism. Surely, we have moved on. Stacy won't stand for it. Stacy!

Karl goes to Stacy.

She wants you to play Malcolm X because you're black.

STACY. Are you serious?

ADRIENNE. Isn't that great, Stacy?

STACY. You want me to play Malcolm X?

ADRIENNE. Yes I do, sister.

STACY. I'm sorry. I can't do it.

KARL. See. It's ridiculous. Asking a woman to play a male part because of the colour of her skin.

STACY. Oh it's not that. It's just ... I'm a pacifist. I won't play terrorists.

ADRIENNE. Whoa!

STACY. What? Malcolm X was a terrorist, right?

KARL. Stacy?!

STACY. By any means necessary. That's what he said. That's terrorism, right? And wasn't he a Muslim?

ADRIENNE. *[to audience]* I am so sorry.

STACY. Malcolm Bin Laden in pantyhose? I don't know if I'm comfortable with that.

KARL. Sweetheart, Malcolm X was a beacon of light, a freedom fighter, and a personal life-long hero of mine!

STACY. I don't know, to me he was just a racist.

ADRIENNE. Whoa! *[to audience]* We do not intend to cause any ...

KARL. Stacy darling, you of all people ... you cannot say that!

STACY. Can't say what?

ADRIENNE. Clare!

CLARE. *[reads]* The producers would like to dissociate themselves from the last comments.

STACY. Malcolm X was against integration, he wanted separation. I don't know, isn't that racism?

KARL. They were different times! Back then, African-Americans suffered terrible racism.

STACY. And we don't have racism today?

KARL. Of course, but it's more tasteful.

STACY. OK, in 1961, Malcolm X spoke here at a Nation of Islam rally, right?

MJ. This is where the Nazi Rockwell listened to Malcolm X.
And gave up twenty dollars to the Nation.
It was a wonderful show.

STACY. When Rockwell put his money on the plate, Malcolm X didn't say: 'Get your Nazi dollars out of my face'. He asked for a round of applause. Hey, doesn't that make Malcolm X a Nazi?

KARL. No, it does not make Malcolm X a Nazi!

ADRIENNE. Clare!

STACY. Relax! I'm just fucking with you!

KARL. Well I don't find it funny.

STACY. Oh come on, you black panther.

KARL. Am I smiling?

STACY. You people need to lighten up.

KARL. You people?

STACY. You people are supposed to have a sense of humour.

KARL. The Irish are some kind of feckin' joke, is that it? We've been fighting this prejudice for years, and I'm telling you, the Irish are not funny!

STACY. That's what I'm talking about!

ADRIENNE. And scene ...

Karl does a dance, angrily, ironically.

KARL. Begorrah! Top of the feckin' morning?! Is that it? Is it?

STACY. I see little people, they're everywhere ...!

KARL. We are not little people!

STACY. I don't know about that.

CHRIS. Oh, it's true.

KARL. Now we see it! The face of racism!

Adrienne has lost control of the group.

ADRIENNE. *[trying to draw it to a close]* And scene ...!

JASON. *[goes to Karl, sings]* We shall overcome, we shall overcome ...!

ADRIENNE. And scene ...!

The actors are now in pairs, arguing, up in each other's faces. It's Nazis versus Nation of Islam. The raucous big band of Flying Home by Duke Ellington starts to play. The couples dance like they hate and love each other at the same time and soon disappear into the darkness, leaving Karl and Stacy the focus of attention. They dance. The music ends. They stare into each other's eyes. Karl tries to kiss Stacy. She slaps him and storms off.

KARL. But I think I love you ...!

Karl exits, following her ...
The space is empty, then ...
In the half dark, a man walks through the space calling out: Rag and Bones!
He disappears into the darkness.
A moment.
Then grainy footage of The Beatles' first American press conference in the Uline appears on the back wall of the arena. We hear the sound of a clamouring press pack.

REPORTER 1. Boys, what do you think of America?

REPORTER 2. What do you think about President Johnson?

REPORTER 3. How do you like American girls?

REPORTER 1. Well what do you think about the assassination of Malcolm X?

REPORTER 2. And what do you think about the assassination of Nazi leader George Lincoln Rockwell?

REPORTER 3. Boys, what do you think about John Lennon's assassination?

REPORTER 1. What do you think about the assassination of John Lennon?

REPORTER 2. The assassination of John Lennon outside the Dakota Building?

REPORTER 3. John?

REPORTER 1. John?

REPORTER 2. John?

The Beatles fade to black.

Clare goes to the audience with her clipboard followed by Adrienne.

CLARE. At this point ... to clarify ... In case you feel confused or short-changed by this ... experience. I've been asked to ... *[reads]* Swampoodle, hereafter referred to as 'the show' or 'Swampoodle' will commence shortly. The producers remind patrons that Swampoodle is not Riverdance, nor is it Lord of the Dance. Swampoodle is less Irish and less comedic than either of those entertainments. Therefore, we cannot take responsibility for any moral compromises, petty crimes, youthful misdemeanours, festering resentments, missed opportunities, ill-advised love affairs or foolish life-choices made by you during Swampoodle. Swampoodle will run and run and run regardless. It is entirely up to patrons to enjoy the show. We cannot enjoy it for you. This is not Riverdance. Nothing is guaranteed. The show goes on. Take from it what you will, before it's too late. Yours. The producers.

ADRIENNE. Yes, thank you Clare. I think that really clarifies a lot of things.

CLARE. What? No.

ADRIENNE. I said, that really clarifies everything, Clare.

CLARE. But ... but ... There's no script! There! We are making it up as we go along!

ADRIENNE. Clare Barrett!

CLARE. *[to audience]* And for all I care you may as well be in this show! You know as much as we do. Go ahead boo, shout, stamp your feet, shake your head, dance, dance, dance! Do something! Whatever it takes to get you through to the other side!

ADRIENNE. Pull yourself together woman! Pull yourself together!

CLARE. But why are we here!?

ADRIENNE. We're here for the show!

CLARE. Adrienne. Give it to me straight. Is there a show?

ADRIENNE. There's a show, of course there's a show.

CLARE. But they *[the audience]* don't know what it's about!

ADRIENNE. Jesus, Clare! They're not stupid!

Adrienne exits, upset.

CLARE. Have you met the writer?! *[to audience]* I met him in a bar on H Street. The man's a clueless feckin' drunk!

MJ passes through.

MJ. Standing on the platform.
Trains keep rolling past.
Down the old Ohio Line.
Disappearing fast.

CLARE. What?

MJ. Ah, just something I'm workin' on.

MJ exits.

CLARE. I'm a stage-manager with no script, no set, no actors. And I'm in a parking lot, at night, in a rundown part of town.

Clare exits.
Jason enters from the far end of the arena.

JASON. Hi. Um ... Because of some stuff that took place earlier, I didn't get a chance to read you this article I found when I was doing my research into Swampoodle. So seeing as there's ... while we're waiting I thought I'd read you this. It's from the Washington Post of 1896 and the article's called: Killed by a Man's Kick, A Saturday night murder in Jackson's Alley. In a section of the city where the respectability of a resident is estimated by the amount of bodily injury he can inflict in a fight: where the alleys show a promiscuous mixing of the white and colored races, and where the people, in clannish brutality, attempt to shield criminals from the law, is located Jackson's alley, which was the scene of a peculiar murder on Saturday night. About 9 o'clock that night, John Mahoney and Patrick Bennett, two Irish labourers, staggered, arm-in-arm, into the alley. The two were returning to their homes in a state of hilarious intoxication. As they passed along singing fragments of songs, a woman selling pieces of pork from a basket passed them, crying out her wares, and attracted the attention of the two men. 'Now' cried Mahoney, 'if there is anything which I like it's a pig's tail, well cooked.' For some reason or other this remark did not seem to strike Bennett's fancy. He replied in a manner at variance with the rules of etiquette. This Mahoney resented, and in a few moments the men were engaged in a dispute ...

Rosy – an elderly homeless woman – emerges from the audience.

ROSY. Life's too short!

JASON. Excuse me?

ROSY. Life's too short!

JASON. OK. Thank you. I'm nearly finished ... and in a few moments the men were engaged in a ...

ROSY. I can't wait around here forever!

JASON. And in a few moments the men were engaged in a ...

Rachel has entered and spotted Rosy.

RACHEL. Oh my God, you made it!

JASON. ... in a dispute.

RACHEL. This is Rosy everyone. Isn't she amazing?

JASON. Rachel, I am reading an article.

ROSY. I thought I was going to pass out.

RACHEL. *[to audience]* We met this morning.

JASON. Rachel?

ROSY. I was outside Starbucks.

JASON. Rachel?!

RACHEL. Jason? Fuck. Like have some ... you know?

ROSY. I was outside Starbucks hustling for quarters.

RACHEL. Yes you were, Rosy. But that's not why we brought you here today, is it?

ROSY. You tell me, Dicky.

RACHEL. We brought you here today because you have a very special link to the Uline, don't you?

ROSY. Yes sir, Dicky.

RACHEL. (It's Rachel, sweety) What was it you used to do here?

ROSY. Used to eat here every day.

RACHEL. Oh ... Right. Here?

ROSY. Best trash transfer centre in the city. A three-course meal in every garbage bag, guaranteed.

RACHEL. OK ... Yes ... But also, Rosy here performed in the opening show here at the Uline Arena. The Icecapades of 1941. Isn't that incredible?

ROSY. That's right, Dicky. Icecapades of 1941. I was a wonderful skater.

RACHEL. And here's a photograph of you Rosy from that very same show.

ROSY. Jesus Christ, I was hot.

RACHEL. Which one is you Rosy?

Adrienne enters, surprised by Rosy's presence.

ROSY. Third from the right, thighs of steel, killer rack.

RACHEL. And what do you remember about that time?

ROSY. I was swatting them away, honey. Buzzing round me like flies round shit, I can tell you.

Adrienne takes Rachel aside. We understand that Adrienne is not impressed by Rosy and wants her removed.

ROSY. Oh, we met lots of famous people. Big names. Big names. Simone Simon, Martha Scott, Lou Holtz, Fred Keating, Betty Field, Jessie Matthews, The Allisons, Wilbur Evans, Gertrude Niesen. We met all the big names.

RACHEL. You must have learned a lot from them.

ROSY. Here's what I got, Dicky. Big names wind up has-beens, has-beens wind up nobodies and nobodies wind up dead. Enjoy life. Grab it by the balls. You'll be dead very soon.

RACHEL. Well thank you for that Rosy ... and for sharing those wonderful memories. What a lady. OK, the real reason we ...

ROSY. I remember this neighbourhood in the 80's, boy was it rough.

RACHEL. Oh my God, drugs were a huge problem in the '80s.

ROSY. Whisky, it was whisky, Dicky. In the 1880's. And they called this place Swampoodle. A cop would risk his nuts coming down here to Jackson Alley. They were big Irish men who knew how to drink and knew how to fight: Dougie McGraw, Mickey McMahon, Tom Farrell, Jimmy Quill, Patrick Ferban, Bill Madden, Bernie Downing, Martin Lane. When men like that walked in the door, the women fainted and the men jumped out the window.

RACHEL. Wow. Big men with big reputations.

ROSY. They're all dead, ain't they?

ADRIENNE. Yes. Wonderful memories. Thank you, Rosy ...

ROSY. I remember when this whole place was just a river and a swamp. The Nacotchtank Indians used to fish here ... when they weren't at war with the Patawomeck or the Susquehannocks, the Iriquois. Of course, then they got massacred by the English. And the rest caught a cold and kicked the bucket.

RACHEL. Thank you Rosy. Thank you so much for sharing. You are such an inspiration ...

Adrienne enters.

ADRIENNE. Yes, thank you. We have a show ... and we're already way behind, so ...

Adrienne puts a dollar in Rosy's hand and starts to lead her away.

RACHEL. Hold on! Rosy wants to sing. Rosy has lived her whole live regretting that she never sang at the Uline.

ROSY. Not a day goes by. I never got the chance.

ADRIENNE. You can sing outside the Uline, can't you Rosy ...?

Rachel brings Rosy back to centre stage. Rachel blocks Adrienne from getting at Rosy.

RACHEL. This isn't your fucking show!

ADRIENNE. We are professionals!

RACHEL. Go ahead sing, Rosy.

ADRIENNE. We don't just bring tramps in off the street.

RACHEL. Haven't you heard of 'Carpe Diem'?

ADRIENNE. If that's one of your drugs, then no.

RACHEL. Do it, Rosy! Sing, Rosy!

ADRIENNE. Do not sing!

RACHEL. Sing!

ROSY. *[sings]* Ol' man river, that ol' man river ...

ADRIENNE. *[storming off]* Security!

ROSY. He must know something but don't say nothing. He just keeps rolling, he keeps on rolling along. He don't plant taters, he don't plant cotton. And them that plants 'em is soon forgotten. But ol' man river he just keeps on rollin' along ...!

After the first verse, a marching band enters playing Ol' Man River. Rosy exits the arena marching at the head of the band. Adrienne can't stop them.

ADRIENNE. Thanks, Rachel! How are we going to do a show with no band?!

RACHEL. Don't lay this on me! I didn't go picking on a defenceless old lady.

ADRIENNE. Defenceless?! She's the pied fucking piper! You know what? I've had enough. This show is cancelled!

RACHEL. You don't fucking cancel the show! You can't do that!

The other cast members enter.

ADRIENNE. It's over. It is over!

RACHEL. Guys, she's trying to cancel the show!

ADRIENNE. I'm cancelling! I am the canceller!

Two rival groups form.

CHRIS. She cannot do this!

STEPHANIE. Who gave you the right, Adrienne?

ADRIENNE. It's over, it's not happening, the show can't go on!

JASON. *[at Rachel, Chris, Stephanie]* This is your fault!

STEPHANIE. *[at Karl, Stacy, Jason]* Our fault?! You people make me sick!

KARL. Here we go again!

STACY. You better watch your mouth!

CHRIS. Or else what!?

JASON. You know what!

The two sides confront each other.
We hear the sound of an excited boxing crowd, the fight bell rings. The two camps go to two 'corners' and huddle. A 'dolly bird' parades a placard which reads Round 1.

ANNOUNCER. Welcome to the world famous U-line parking lot! Formerly DC's premier trash transfer centre ... Formerly The Miracle Faith Centre. Formerly the Washington Coliseum. Formerly the Uline Arena. Formerly the Irish shantytown Swampoodle. Formerly a swamp on the banks of Tiber Creek. Formerly known as Goose Creek. Formerly known by its Native American name, which has been forgotten.

CO-ANNOUNCER. Wiped off the face of the earth, Jim.

ANNOUNCER. Just like the Nacotchtank Indians who lived in these parts.

CO-ANNOUNCER. *[laughs]* Formerly.

ANNOUNCER. Ladies and gentlemen welcome to Swampoodle! And here they come ... Bennett and Mahoney.

The two men enter. Chris plays Bennett and Jason plays Mahoney. They are followed by their corner men and supporters perhaps. They warm up in their corners and get advice from their teams.

CO-ANNOUNCER. What a night, Jim.

ANNOUNCER. What a night.

CO-ANNOUNCER. Do you know Jim, I was thinking on the way over.

ANNOUNCER. Good for you.

CO-ANNOUNCER. Tonight's all about life, isn't it?

ANNOUNCER. For sure. And death, right?

CO-ANNOUNCER. Life and death. You got it, Jim.

ANNOUNCER. OK then, I know this one's closer than a cutthroat but I'm going to ask you to call it.

CO-ANNOUNCER. Call me crazy, Jim, but I'm calling it for hope. My money's on hope, in the fifteenth.

ANNOUNCER. Hope in the fifteenth round. Bloodied and bruised and half-blind hope ... So what do we know about these two men, Bennett and Mahoney?

CO-ANNOUNCER. What can I tell you, Jim? Both men hail from Jackson's Alley, Swampoodle. And both training out of Sullivan's Whiskey Saloon.

ANNOUNCER. So they're friends?

CO-ANNOUNCER. That's right, Jim. But hold on ... Mahoney's made a comment about pig tails. Mahoney likes 'em well cooked.

ANNOUNCER. Strange way to start a fight.

Chris/Bennett and Jason/Mahoney circle each other.

CO-ANNOUNCER. Men have died for less, Jim.

ANNOUNCER. Bennett is not happy.

CO-ANNOUNCER. He's come back with jab or a jibe or ...

ANNOUNCER. ... Something about pigs ...

CO-ANNOUNCER. And Mahoney's mentioned his mother!

ANNOUNCER. He's mentioned his mother!

Jason/Mahoney lands a blow on Chris/Bennett. The fight kicks off.

CO-ANNOUNCER. We've got a street fight on our hands!

ANNOUNCER. The crowd are loving it!

CO-ANNOUNCER. This is what they came to see!

ANNOUNCER. This is what tonight's all about!

CO-ANNOUNCER. Oh my, absolutely senseless!

ANNOUNCER. And that's exactly what tonight is ...

Jason hits Chris hard.

CO-ANNOUNCER. He's hurt! Bennett's hurt!

Chris stumbles away and falls.
Jason stamps on Chris's head.
Jason runs off, the lights flicker.

ANNOUNCER. Bennett's down. He's down. Something's wrong ...

ADRIENNE. Somebody!

The announcers' microphone dies. The arena's plunged into semi darkness.

ANNOUNCER. Something's wrong ...

ADRIENNE. Please!

CO-ANNOUNCER. Something's very wrong ...

ADRIENNE. Please! Somebody!

There's an air of panic in the semi-darkness. Adrienne comes to the audience. Close to tears, Adrienne can't speak. Clare looks through the papers on her clipboard, drops it on the floor. They exit and Stacy comes forward to the audience.

STACY. Ladies and gentlemen.
At times like these ... When you least expect.
We wish we could again, go back.
But no.
At times ...
We hope you'll ...
We are only human.
Sometimes.
We forget.

Karl goes to Stacy who turns to Karl. He takes her hand and they walk into the dark. The following is sung by all, almost like a spiritual song.

We're all trash men.
We're all clowns.
We're all drunks.

We're all B-list celebrities.
We're all soldiers.
We're all women of the night.
We're all moneymen.
We're all race-haters.
We're all rodeo riders.
We're all chorus girls.
We're all railroad men.
We're all here, now.
We're all here, now.
We're all here.

The following is spoken over the song, almost like a preacher.

MJ. We are gathered here today.
In a rundown part of town.
Trains go by, trains go by.
We are gathered here today.
In a rundown part of town.
A river underneath our feet.
We are gathered here today.
In a rundown part of town.
The show goes on and on.

One by one, the other performers exit.

MJ is back at the spot where he began the play. He sweeps, raising a cloud of white dust. On the cathedral-like roof of the arena, a series of black and white moving images are projected. Boxers fight, Nureyev dances, worshippers clap their hands, The Beatles play, Malcolm X speaks to the crowd ...

MJ exits.
A moment of quiet.
In the darkness, Adrienne and Clare enter like it's the first time they've ever seen the audience.

ADRIENNE. *[nervous, in the dark]* Hello?! Who's there?!

A light goes on illuminating the audience.

What are you doing here?

CLARE. *[prompting]* Who's here for Swampoodle?

ADRIENNE. *[enthusiastically]* Who's here for Swampoodle?!

CLARE. *[whispers loudly into her walkie-talkie]* Standby ...

ADRIENNE. Hands up!

CLARE. Standby Music 1 ...

ADRIENNE. Yes, yes ... We're all here now.

CLARE. Music 1, Go.

The big band jazz of Apple Honey by Woody Herman fills the arena.

Clare and Adrienne usher the audience towards the exit door.

ADRIENNE. We're all here for the show.

CLARE. Standby Lights 1 ...

ADRIENNE. How wonderful, yes ... We're all here.

CLARE. Lights 1, Go!

Bright lights illuminate the rest of the cast. It's an MGM Musical moment – the performers flank either side of the exit adorned with ostrich feathers and big smiles. Behind them, big red curtains hang in front of the exit.

ADRIENNE. Ladies and gentlemen, in the unlikely event of a show ...

KARL. Please make sure that your mind is securely fastened ...

STACY. As it may move about during the trip ...

MJ. Causing a hazard to yourself and others.

RACHEL. It's a wonderful show!

CHRIS. Ladies and gentlemen, please take a moment to reflect on past mistakes ...

CLARE. And prepare to repeat them ...

STEPHANIE. Over and over ...

JASON. It's a wonderful show!

The cast guide the audience towards the exit door, which is starting to open.

ADRIENNE. Ladies and gentlemen, please remain on your feet during take-off ...

KARL. Because life is short ...

STACY. And must be lived one day at a time!

MJ. It's a wonderful show!

A red carpet is rolled out for the audience.

RACHEL. Ladies and gentlemen, we cannot take responsibility ...

CHRIS. We did not write this ...

CLARE. You are the authors ...

STEPHANIE. Of your own destiny!

JASON. It's a wonderful show!

The curtains open to reveal the world outside.
The cast gesture theatrically towards the exit.

ALL. It's a wonderful show!
Ladies and gentlemen, we give you ... SWAMPOODLE!

Carysfort Press was formed in the summer of 1998. It receives annual funding from the Arts Council.

The directors believe that drama is playing an ever-increasing role in today's society and that enjoyment of the theatre, both professional and amateur, currently plays a central part in Irish culture.

The Press aims to produce high quality publications which, though written and/or edited by academics, will be made accessible to a general readership. The organisation would also like to provide a forum for critical thinking in the Arts in Ireland, again keeping the needs and interests of the general public in view.

The company publishes contemporary Irish writing for and about the theatre.

Editorial and publishing inquiries to:
Carysfort Press Ltd.,
58 Woodfield,
Scholarstown Road,
Rathfarnham,
Dublin 16,
Republic of Ireland.

T (353 1) 493 7383
F (353 1) 406 9815
E: info@carysfortpress.com
www.carysfortpress.com

HOW TO ORDER

TRADE ORDERS DIRECTLY TO:
Irish Book Distribution
Unit 12, North Park, North Road,
Finglas, Dublin 11.

T: (353 1) 8239580
F: (353 1) 8239599
E: mary@argosybooks.ie
www.argosybooks.ie

INDIVIDUAL ORDERS DIRECTLY TO:
eprint Ltd.
35 Coolmine Industrial Estate,
Blanchardstown, Dublin 15.
T: (353 1) 827 8860
F: (353 1) 827 8804 Order online @
E: books@eprint.ie
www.eprint.ie

FOR SALES IN NORTH AMERICA AND CANADA:
Dufour Editions Inc.,
124 Byers Road,
PO Box 7,
Chester Springs,
PA 19425,
USA

T: 1-610-458-5005
F: 1-610-458-7103

Synge and His Influences: Centenary Essays from the Synge Summer School

Edited by Patrick Lonergan

The year 2009 was the centenary of the death of John Millington Synge, one of the world's great dramatists. To mark the occasion, this book gathers essays by leading scholars of Irish drama, aiming to explore the writers and movements that shaped Synge, and to consider his enduring legacies. Essays discuss Synge's work in its Irish, European and world contexts – showing his engagement not just with the Irish literary revival but with European politics and culture too. The book also explores Synge's influence on later writers: Irish dramatists such as Brian Friel, Tom Murphy and Marina Carr, as well as international writers like Mustapha Matura and Erisa Kironde. It also considers Synge's place in Ireland today, revealing how *The Playboy of the Western World* has helped to shape Ireland's responses to globalisation and multiculturalism, in celebrated productions by the Abbey Theatre, Druid Theatre, and Pan Pan Theatre Company.

Contributors include Ann Saddlemyer, Ben Levitas, Mary Burke, Paige Reynolds, Eilís Ní Dhuibhne, Mark Phelan, Shaun Richards, Ondřej Pilný, Richard Pine, Alexandra Poulain, Emilie Pine, Melissa Sihra, Sara Keating, Bisi Adigun, Adrian Frazier and Anthony Roche.

ISBN: 978-1-904505-50-1 €20.00

Constellations - The Life and Music of John Buckley

Benjamin Dwyer

Benjamin Dwyer provides a long overdue assessment of one of Ireland's most prolific composers of the last decades. He looks at John Buckley's music in the context of his biography and Irish cultural life. This is no hagiography but a critical assessment of Buckley's work, his roots and aesthetics. While looking closely at several of Buckley's compositions, the book is written in a comprehensible style that makes it easily accessible to anybody interested in Irish musical and cultural history. *Wolfgang Marx*

As well as providing a very readable and comprehensive study of the life and music of John Buckley, Constellations also offers an up-to-date and informative catalogue of compositions, a complete discography, translations of set texts and the full libretto of his chamber opera, making this book an essential guide for both students and professional scholars alike.

ISBN: 978-1-904505-52-5 €20.00

'Because We Are Poor':
Irish Theatre in the 1990s

Victor Merriman

"Victor Merriman's work on Irish theatre is in the vanguard of a whole new paradigm in Irish theatre scholarship, one that is not content to contemplate monuments of past or present achievement, but for which the theatre is a lens that makes visible the hidden malaises in Irish society. That he has been able to do so by focusing on a period when so much else in Irish culture conspired to hide those problems is only testimony to the considerable power of his critical scrutiny." Chris Morash, NUI Maynooth.

ISBN: 978-1-904505-51-8 €20.00

'Buffoonery and Easy Sentiment':
Popular Irish Plays in the Decade Prior to the Opening of The Abbey Theatre

Christopher Fitz-Simon

In this fascinating reappraisal of the non-literary drama of the late 19th - early 20th century, Christopher Fitz-Simon discloses a unique world of plays, players and producers in metropolitan theatres in Ireland and other countries where Ireland was viewed as a source of extraordinary topics at once contemporary and comfortably remote: revolution, eviction, famine, agrarian agitation, political assassination.

The form was the fashionable one of melodrama, yet Irish melodrama was of a particular kind replete with hidden messages, and the language was far more allusive, colourful and entertaining than that of its English equivalent.

ISBN: 978-1-9045505-49-5 €20.00

The Fourth Seamus Heaney Lectures, 'Mirror up to Nature':

Ed. Patrick Burke

What, in particular, is the contemporary usefulness for the building of societies of one of our oldest and culturally valued ideals, that of drama? The Fourth Seamus Heaney Lectures, 'Mirror up to Nature': Drama and Theatre in the Modern World, given at St Patrick's College, Drumcondra, between October 2006 and April 2007, addressed these and related questions. Patrick Mason spoke on the essence of theatre, Thomas Kilroy on Ireland's contribution to the art of theatre, Cecily O'Neill and Jonothan Neelands on the rich potential of drama in the classroom. Brenna Katz Clarke examined the relationship between drama and film, and John Buckley spoke on opera and its history and gave an illuminating account of his own *Words Upon The Window-Pane*.

ISBN 978-1-9045505-48-8 €12

The Theatre of Tom Mac Intyre: 'Strays from the ether'

Eds. Bernadette Sweeney and Marie Kelly

This long overdue anthology captures the soul of Mac Intyre's dramatic canon – its ethereal qualities, its extraordinary diversity, its emphasis on the poetic and on performance – in an extensive range of visual, journalistic and scholarly contributions from writers, theatre practitioners.

ISBN 978-1-904505-46-4 €25

Irish Appropriation Of Greek Tragedy

Brian Arkins

This book presents an analysis of more than 30 plays written by Irish dramatists and poets that are based on the tragedies of Sophocles, Euripides and Aeschylus. These plays proceed from the time of Yeats and Synge through MacNeice and the Longfords on to many of today's leading writers.

ISBN 978-1-904505-47-1 €20

Alive in Time: The Enduring Drama of Tom Murphy

Ed. Christopher Murray

Almost 50 years after he first hit the headlines as Ireland's most challenging playwright, the 'angry young man' of those times Tom Murphy still commands his place at the pinnacle of Irish theatre. Here 17 new essays by prominent critics and academics, with an introduction by Christopher Murray, survey Murphy's dramatic oeuvre in a concerted attempt to define his greatness and enduring appeal, making this book a significant study of a unique genius.

ISBN 978-1-904505-45-7 €25

Performing Violence in Contemporary Ireland

Ed. Lisa Fitzpatrick

This interdisciplinary collection of fifteen new essays by scholars of theatre, Irish studies, music, design and politics explores aspects of the performance of violence in contemporary Ireland. With chapters on the work of playwrights Martin McDonagh, Martin Lynch, Conor McPherson and Gary Mitchell, on Republican commemorations and the 90th anniversary ceremonies for the Battle of the Somme and the Easter Rising, this book aims to contribute to the ongoing international debate on the performance of violence in contemporary societies.

ISBN 978-1-904505-44-0 (2009) €20

Ireland's Economic Crisis - Time to Act. Essays from over 40 leading Irish thinkers at the MacGill Summer School 2009

Eds. Joe Mulholland and Finbarr Bradley

Ireland's economic crisis requires a radical transformation in policymaking. In this volume, political, industrial, academic, trade union and business leaders and commentators tell the story of the Irish economy and its rise and fall. Contributions at Glenties range from policy, vision and context to practical suggestions on how the country can emerge from its crisis.

ISBN 978-1-904505-43-3 (2009) €20

Deviant Acts: Essays on Queer Performance

Ed. David Cregan

This book contains an exciting collection of essays focusing on a variety of alternative performances happening in contemporary Ireland. While it highlights the particular representations of gay and lesbian identity it also brings to light how diversity has always been a part of Irish culture and is, in fact, shaping what it means to be Irish today.

ISBN 978-1-904505-42-6 (2009) €20

Seán Keating in Context: Responses to Culture and Politics in Post-Civil War Ireland

Compiled, edited and introduced by Éimear O'Connor

Irish artist Seán Keating has been judged by his critics as the personification of old-fashioned traditionalist values. This book presents a different view. The story reveals Keating's early determination to attain government support for the visual arts. It also illustrates his socialist leanings, his disappointment with capitalism, and his attitude to cultural snobbery, to art critics, and to the Academy. Given the national and global circumstances nowadays, Keating's critical and wry observations are prophetic – and highly amusing.

ISBN 978-1-904505-41-9 €25

Dialogue of the Ancients of Ireland: A new translation of Acallam na Senorach

Translated with introduction and notes by Maurice Harmon

One of Ireland's greatest collections of stories and poems, The Dialogue of the Ancients of Ireland is a new translation by Maurice Harmon of the 12th century *Acallam na Senorach*. Retold in a refreshing modern idiom, the *Dialogue* is an extraordinary account of journeys to the four provinces by St. Patrick and the pagan Cailte, one of the surviving Fian. Within the frame story are over 200 other stories reflecting many genres – wonder tales, sea journeys, romances, stories of revenge, tales of monsters and magic. The poems are equally varied – lyrics, nature poems, eulogies, prophecies, laments, genealogical poems. After the *Tain Bo Cuailnge*, the *Acallam* is the largest surviving prose work in Old and Middle Irish.

ISBN: 978-1-904505-39-6 (2009) €20

Literary and Cultural Relations between Ireland and Hungary and Central and Eastern Europe

Ed. Maria Kurdi

This lively, informative and incisive collection of essays sheds fascinating new light on the literary interrelations between Ireland, Hungary, Poland, Romania and the Czech Republic. It charts a hitherto under-explored history of the reception of modern Irish culture in Central and Eastern Europe and also investigates how key authors have been translated, performed and adapted. The revealing explorations undertaken in this volume of a wide array of Irish dramatic and literary texts, ranging from *Gulliver's Travels* to *Translations* and *The Pillowman*, tease out the subtly altered nuances that they acquire in a Central European context.

ISBN: 978-1-904505-40-2 (2009) €20

Plays and Controversies: Abbey Theatre Diaries 2000-2005

Ben Barnes

In diaries covering the period of his artistic directorship of the Abbey, Ben Barnes offers a frank, honest, and probing account of a much commented upon and controversial period in the history of the national theatre. These diaries also provide fascinating personal insights into the day-to- day pressures, joys, and frustrations of running one of Ireland's most iconic institutions.

ISBN: 978-1-904505-38-9 (2008) €35

Interactions: Dublin Theatre Festival 1957-2007. Irish Theatrical Diaspora Series: 3

Eds. Nicholas Grene and Patrick Lonergan with Lilian Chambers

For over 50 years the Dublin Theatre Festival has been one of Ireland's most important cultural events, bringing countless new Irish plays to the world stage, while introducing Irish audiences to the most important international theatre companies and artists. Interactions explores and celebrates the achievements of the renowned Festival since 1957 and includes specially commissioned memoirs from past organizers, offering a unique perspective on the controversies and successes that have marked the event's history. An especially valuable feature of the volume, also, is a complete listing of the shows that have appeared at the Festival from 1957 to 2008.

ISBN: 978-1-904505-36-5 €25

The Informer: A play by Tom Murphy based on the novel by Liam O'Flaherty

The Informer, Tom Murphy's stage adaptation of Liam O'Flaherty's novel, was produced in the 1981 Dublin Theatre Festival, directed by the playwright himself, with Liam Neeson in the leading role. The central subject of the play is the quest of a character at the point of emotional and moral breakdown for some source of meaning or identity. In the case of Gypo Nolan, the informer of the title, this involves a nightmarish progress through a Dublin underworld in which he changes from a Judas figure to a scapegoat surrogate for Jesus, taking upon himself the sins of the world. A cinematic style, with flash-back and intercut scenes, is used rather than a conventional theatrical structure to catch the fevered and phantasmagoric progression of Gypo's mind. The language, characteristically for Murphy, mixes graphically colloquial Dublin slang with the haunted intricacies of the central character groping for the meaning of his own actions. The dynamic rhythm of the action builds towards an inevitable but theatrically satisfying tragic catastrophe. ' [The Informer] is, in many ways closer to being an original Murphy play than it is to O'Flaherty...' Fintan O'Toole.

ISBN: 978-1-904505-37-2 (2008) €10

Shifting Scenes: Irish theatre-going 1955-1985

Eds. Nicholas Grene and Chris Morash

Transcript of conversations with John Devitt, academic and reviewer, about his lifelong passion for the theatre. A fascinating and entertaining insight into Dublin theatre over the course of thirty years provided by Devitt's vivid reminiscences and astute observations.

ISBN: 978-1-904505-33-4 (2008) €10

Irish Literature: Feminist Perspectives

Eds. Patricia Coughlan and Tina O'Toole

The collection discusses texts from the early 18th century to the present. A central theme of the book is the need to renegotiate the relations of feminism with nationalism and to transact the potential contest of these two important narratives, each possessing powerful emancipatory force. Irish Literature: Feminist Perspectives contributes incisively to contemporary debates about Irish culture, gender and ideology.

ISBN: 978-1-904505-35-8 (2008) €25

Silenced Voices: Hungarian Plays from Transylvania

Selected and translated by Csilla Bertha and Donald E. Morse

The five plays are wonderfully theatrical, moving fluidly from absurdism to tragedy, and from satire to the darkly comic. Donald Morse and Csilla Bertha's translations capture these qualities perfectly, giving voice to the 'forgotten playwrights of Central Europe'. They also deeply enrich our understanding of the relationship between art, ethics, and politics in Europe.

ISBN: 978-1-904505-34-1 (2008) €25

A Hazardous Melody of Being:
Seóirse Bodley's Song Cycles on the poems of Micheal O'Siadhail

Ed. Lorraine Byrne Bodley

This apograph is the first publication of Bodley's O'Siadhail song cycles and is the first book to explore the composer's lyrical modernity from a number of perspectives. Lorraine Byrne Bodley's insightful introduction describes in detail the development and essence of Bodley's musical thinking, the European influences he absorbed which linger in these cycles, and the importance of his work as a composer of the Irish art song.

ISBN: 978-1-904505-31-0 (2008) €25

Irish Theatre in England: Irish Theatrical Diaspora Series: 2

Eds. Richard Cave and Ben Levitas

Irish theatre in England has frequently illustrated the complex relations between two distinct cultures. How English reviewers and audiences interpret Irish plays is often decidedly different from how the plays were read in performance in Ireland. How certain Irish performers have chosen to be understood in Dublin is not necessarily how audiences in London have perceived their constructed stage personae. Though a collection by diverse authors, the twelve essays in this volume investigate these issues from a variety of perspectives that together chart the trajectory of Irish performance in England from the mid-nineteenth century till today.

ISBN: 978-1-904505-26-6 (2007) €20

Goethe and Anna Amalia: A Forbidden Love?

Ettore Ghibellino, Trans. Dan Farrelly

In this study Ghibellino sets out to show that the platonic relationship between Goethe and Charlotte von Stein – lady-in-waiting to Anna Amalia, the Dowager Duchess of Weimar – was used as part of a cover-up for Goethe's intense and prolonged love relationship with the Duchess Anna Amalia herself. The book attempts to uncover a hitherto closely-kept state secret. Readers convinced by the evidence supporting Ghibellino's hypothesis will see in it one of the very great love stories in European history – to rank with that of Dante and Beatrice, and Petrarch and Laura.

ISBN: 978-1-904505-24-2 €20

Ireland on Stage: Beckett and After

Eds. Hiroko Mikami, Minako Okamuro, Naoko Yagi

The collection focuses primarily on Irish playwrights and their work, both in text and on the stage during the latter half of the twentieth century. The central figure is Samuel Beckett, but the contributors freely draw on Beckett and his work provides a springboard to discuss contemporary playwrights such as Brian Friel, Frank McGuinness, Marina Carr and Conor McPherson amongst others. Contributors include: Anthony Roche, Hiroko Mikami, Naoko Yagi, Cathy Leeney, Joseph Long, Noreem Doody, Minako Okamuro, Christopher Murray, Futoshi Sakauchi and Declan Kiberd

ISBN: 978-1-904505-23-5 (2007) €20

'Echoes Down the Corridor': Irish Theatre - Past, Present and Future

Eds. Patrick Lonergan and Riana O'Dwyer

This collection of fourteen new essays explores Irish theatre from exciting new perspectives. How has Irish theatre been received internationally - and, as the country becomes more multicultural, how will international theatre influence the development of drama in Ireland? These and many other important questions.

ISBN: 978-1-904505-25-9 (2007) €20

Musics of Belonging: The Poetry of Micheal O'Siadhail

Eds. Marc Caball & David F. Ford

An overall account is given of O'Siadhail's life, his work and the reception of his poetry so far. There are close readings of some poems, analyses of his artistry in matching diverse content with both classical and innovative forms, and studies of recurrent themes such as love, death, language, music, and the shifts of modern life.

ISBN: 978-1-904505-22-8 (2007) €25 (Paperback)
ISBN: 978-1-904505-21-1 (2007) €50 (Casebound)

Brian Friel's Dramatic Artistry: 'The Work has Value'

Eds. Donald E. Morse, Csilla Bertha and Maria Kurdi

Brian Friel's Dramatic Artistry presents a refreshingly broad range of voices: new work from some of the leading English-speaking authorities on Friel, and fascinating essays from scholars in Germany, Italy, Portugal, and Hungary. This book will deepen our knowledge and enjoyment of Friel's work.

ISBN: 978-1-904505-17-4 (2006) €30

The Theatre of Martin McDonagh: 'A World of Savage Stories'

Eds. Lilian Chambers and Eamonn Jordan

The book is a vital response to the many challenges set by McDonagh for those involved in the production and reception of his work. Critics and commentators from around the world offer a diverse range of often provocative approaches. What is not surprising is the focus and commitment of the engagement, given the controversial and stimulating nature of the work.

ISBN: 978-1-904505-19-8 (2006) €35

Edna O'Brien: New Critical Perspectives

Eds. Kathryn Laing, Sinead Mooney and Maureen O'Connor

The essays collected here illustrate some of the range, complexity, and interest of Edna O'Brien as a fiction writer and dramatist. They will contribute to a broader appreciation of her work and to an evolution of new critical approaches, as well as igniting more interest in the many unexplored areas of her considerable oeuvre.

ISBN: 978-1-904505-20-4 (2006) €20

Irish Theatre on Tour

Eds. Nicholas Grene and Chris Morash

'Touring has been at the strategic heart of Druid's artistic policy since the early eighties. Everyone has the right to see professional theatre in their own communities. Irish theatre on tour is a crucial part of Irish theatre as a whole'. Garry Hynes

ISBN 978-1-904505-13-6 (2005) €20

Poems 2000-2005 by Hugh Maxton

Poems 2000-2005 is a transitional collection written while the author – also known to be W.J. Mc Cormack, literary historian – was in the process of moving back from London to settle in rural Ireland.

ISBN 978-1-904505-12-9 (2005) €10

Synge: A Celebration

Ed. Colm Tóibín

A collection of essays by some of Ireland's most creative writers on the work of John Millington Synge, featuring Sebastian Barry, Marina Carr, Anthony Cronin, Roddy Doyle, Anne Enright, Hugo Hamilton, Joseph O'Connor, Mary O'Malley, Fintan O'Toole, Colm Toibin, Vincent Woods.

ISBN 978-1-904505-14-3 (2005) €15

East of Eden: New Romanian Plays

Ed. Andrei Marinescu

Four of the most promising Romanian playwrights, young and very young, are in this collection, each one with a specific way of seeing the Romanian reality, each one with a style of communicating an articulated artistic vision of the society we are living in. Ion Caramitru, General Director Romanian National Theatre Bucharest.
ISBN 978-1-904505-15-0 (2005) €10

George Fitzmaurice: 'Wild in His Own Way', Biography of an Irish Playwright

Fiona Brennan

'Fiona Brennan's introduction to his considerable output allows us a much greater appreciation and understanding of Fitzmaurice, the one remaining under-celebrated genius of twentieth-century Irish drama'. Conall Morrison

ISBN 978-1-904505-16-7 (2005) €20

Out of History: Essays on the Writings of Sebastian Barry

Ed. Christina Hunt Mahony

The essays address Barry's engagement with the contemporary cultural debate in Ireland and also with issues that inform postcolonial critical theory. The range and selection of contributors has ensured a high level of critical expression and an insightful assessment of Barry and his works.

ISBN: 978-1-904505-18-1 (2005) €20

Three Congregational Masses

Seoirse Bodley

'From the simpler congregational settings in the Mass of Peace and the Mass of Joy to the richer textures of the Mass of Glory, they are immediately attractive and accessible, and with a distinctively Irish melodic quality.' Barra Boydell

ISBN: 978-1-904505-11-2 (2005) €15

Georg Büchner's Woyzeck,

A new translation by Dan Farrelly

The most up-to-date German scholarship of Thomas Michael Mayer and Burghard Dedner has finally made it possible to establish an authentic sequence of scenes. The wide-spread view that this play is a prime example of loose, open theatre is no longer sustainable. Directors and teachers are challenged to "read it again".

ISBN: 978-1-904505-02-0 (2004) €10

Playboys of the Western World: Production Histories

Ed. Adrian Frazier

'The book is remarkably well-focused: half is a series of production histories of Playboy performances through the twentieth century in the UK, Northern Ireland, the USA, and Ireland. The remainder focuses on one contemporary performance, that of Druid Theatre, as directed by Garry Hynes. The various contemporary social issues that are addressed in relation to Synge's play and this performance of it give the volume an additional interest: it shows how the arts matter.' Kevin Barry

ISBN: 978-1-904505-06-8 (2004) €20

The Power of Laughter: Comedy and Contemporary Irish Theatre

Ed. Eric Weitz

The collection draws on a wide range of perspectives and voices including critics, playwrights, directors and performers. The result is a series of fascinating and provocative debates about the myriad functions of comedy in contemporary Irish theatre. Anna McMullan

As Stan Laurel said, 'it takes only an onion to cry. Peel it and weep. Comedy is harder'. 'These essays listen to the power of laughter. They hear the tough heart of Irish theatre – hard and wicked and funny'. Frank McGuinness

ISBN: 978-1-904505-05-1 (2004) €20

Sacred Play: Soul-Journeys in contemporary Irish Theatre

Anne F. O'Reilly

'Theatre as a space or container for sacred play allows audiences to glimpse mystery and to experience transformation. This book charts how Irish playwrights negotiate the labyrinth of the Irish soul and shows how their plays contribute to a poetics of Irish culture that enables a new imagining. Playwrights discussed are: McGuinness, Murphy, Friel, Le Marquand Hartigan, Burke Brogan, Harding, Meehan, Carr, Parker, Devlin, and Barry.'

ISBN: 978-1-904505-07-5 (2004) €25

The Irish Harp Book

Sheila Larchet Cuthbert

This is a facsimile of the edition originally published by Mercier Press in 1993. There is a new preface by Sheila Larchet Cuthbert, and the biographical material has been updated. It is a collection of studies and exercises for the use of teachers and pupils of the Irish harp.
ISBN: 978-1-904505-08-2 (2004) €35

The Drunkard

Tom Murphy

'The Drunkard is a wonderfully eloquent play. Murphy's ear is finely attuned to the glories and absurdities of melodramatic exclamation, and even while he is wringing out its ludicrous overstatement, he is also making it sing.' The Irish Times

ISBN: 978-1-90 05-09-9 (2004) €10

Goethe: Musical Poet, Musical Catalyst

Ed. Lorraine Byrne

'Goethe was interested in, and acutely aware of, the place of music in human experience generally - and of its particular role in modern culture. Moreover, his own literary work - especially the poetry and Faust - inspired some of the major composers of the European tradition to produce some of their finest works.' Martin Swales

ISBN: 978-1-9045-10-5 (2004) €40

The Theatre of Marina Carr: "Before rules was made"

Eds. Anna McMullan & Cathy Leeney

As the first published collection of articles on the theatre of Marina Carr, this volume explores the world of Carr's theatrical imagination, the place of her plays in contemporary theatre in Ireland and abroad and the significance of her highly individual voice.

ISBN: 978-0-9534257-7-8 (2003) €20

Critical Moments: Fintan O'Toole on Modern Irish Theatre

Eds. Julia Furay & Redmond O'Hanlon

This new book on the work of Fintan O'Toole, the internationally acclaimed theatre critic and cultural commentator, offers percussive analyses and assessments of the major plays and playwrights in the canon of modern Irish theatre. Fearless and provocative in his judgements, O'Toole is essential reading for anyone interested in criticism or in the current state of Irish theatre.

ISBN: 978-1-904505-03-7 (2003) €20

Goethe and Schubert: Across the Divide

Eds. Lorraine Byrne & Dan Farrelly

Proceedings of the International Conference, 'Goethe and Schubert in Perspective and Performance', Trinity College Dublin, 2003. This volume includes essays by leading scholars – Barkhoff, Boyle, Byrne, Canisius, Dürr, Fischer, Hill, Kramer, Lamport, Lund, Meikle, Newbould, Norman McKay, White, Whitton, Wright, Youens – on Goethe's musicality and his relationship to Schubert; Schubert's contribution to sacred music and the Lied and his setting of Goethe's Singspiel, Claudine. A companion volume of this Singspiel (with piano reduction and English translation) is also available.

ISBN: 978-1-904505-04-4 (2003) €25

Goethe's Singspiel, 'Claudine von Villa Bella'

Set by Franz Schubert

Goethe's Singspiel in three acts was set to music by Schubert in 1815. Only Act One of Schuberts's Claudine score is extant. The present volume makes Act One available for performance in English and German. It comprises both a piano reduction by Lorraine Byrne of the original Schubert orchestral score and a bilingual text translated for the modern stage by Dan Farrelly. This is a tale, wittily told, of lovers and vagabonds, romance, reconciliation, and resolution of family conflict.

ISBN: 978-0-9544290-0-3 (2002) €20

Theatre of Sound, Radio and the Dramatic Imagination

Dermot Rattigan

An innovative study of the challenges that radio drama poses to the creative imagination of the writer, the production team, and the listener.
"A remarkably fine study of radio drama – everywhere informed by the writer's professional experience of such drama in the making…A new theoretical and analytical approach – informative, illuminating and at all times readable." Richard Allen Cave

ISBN: 978- 0-9534-257-5-4 (2002) €20

Talking about Tom Murphy

Ed. Nicholas Grene

Talking About Tom Murphy is shaped around the six plays in the landmark Abbey Theatre Murphy Season of 2001, assembling some of the best-known commentators on his work: Fintan O'Toole, Chris Morash, Lionel Pilkington, Alexandra Poulain, Shaun Richards, Nicholas Grene and Declan Kiberd.

ISBN: 978-0-9534-257-9-2 (2002) €15

Hamlet: The Shakespearean Director

Mike Wilcock

"This study of the Shakespearean director as viewed through various interpretations of HAMLET is a welcome addition to our understanding of how essential it is for a director to have a clear vision of a great play. It is an important study from which all of us who love Shakespeare and who understand the importance of continuing contemporary exploration may gain new insights." From the Foreword, by Joe Dowling, Artistic Director, The Guthrie Theater, Minneapolis, MN

ISBN: 978-1-904505-00-6 (2002) €20

The Theatre of Frank Mc Guinness: Stages of Mutability

Ed. Helen Lojek

The first edited collection of essays about internationally renowned Irish playwright Frank McGuinness focuses on both performance and text. Interpreters come to diverse conclusions, creating a vigorous dialogue that enriches understanding and reflects a strong consensus about the value of McGuinness's complex work.

ISBN: 978-1904505-01-3. (2002) €20

Theatre Talk: Voices of Irish Theatre Practitioners

Eds Lilian Chambers, Ger Fitzgibbon and Eamonn Jordan

"This book is the right approach - asking practitioners what they feel." Sebastian Barry, Playwright "... an invaluable and informative collection of interviews with those who make and shape the landscape of Irish Theatre." Ben Barnes, Artistic Director of the Abbey Theatre

ISBN: 978-0-9534-257-6-1 (2001) €20

In Search of the South African Iphigenie

Erika von Wietersheim and Dan Farrelly

Discussions of Goethe's "Iphigenie auf Tauris" (Under the Curse) as relevant to women's issues in modern South Africa: women in family and public life; the force of women's spirituality; experience of personal relationships; attitudes to parents and ancestors; involvement with religion.

ISBN: 978-0-9534257-8-5 (2001) €10

'The Starving' and 'October Song':

Two contemporary Irish plays by Andrew Hinds

The Starving, set during and after the siege of Derry in 1689, is a moving and engrossing drama of the emotional journey of two men.

October Song, a superbly written family drama set in real time in pre-ceasefire Derry.

ISBN: 978-0-9534-257-4-7 (2001) €10

Seen and Heard: Six new plays by Irish women

Ed. Cathy Leeney

A rich and funny, moving and theatrically exciting collection of plays by Mary Elizabeth Burke-Kennedy, Síofra Campbell, Emma Donoghue, Anne Le Marquand Hartigan, Michelle Read and Dolores Walshe.

ISBN: 978-0-9534-257-3-0 (2001) €20

Theatre Stuff: Critical essays on contemporary Irish theatre

Ed. Eamonn Jordan

Best selling essays on the successes and debates of contemporary Irish theatre at home and abroad. Contributors include: Thomas Kilroy, Declan Hughes, Anna McMullan, Declan Kiberd, Deirdre Mulrooney, Fintan O'Toole, Christopher Murray, Caoimhe McAvinchey and Terry Eagleton.

ISBN: 978-0-9534-2571-1-6 (2000) €20

Under the Curse. Goethe's "Iphigenie Auf Tauris", A New Version

Dan Farrelly

The Greek myth of Iphigenie grappling with the curse on the house of Atreus is brought vividly to life. This version is currently being used in Johannesburg to explore problems of ancestry, religion, and Black African women's spirituality.

ISBN: 978-09534-257-8-5 (2000) €10

Urfaust, A New Version of Goethe's early "Faust" in Brechtian Mode

Dan Farrelly

This version is based on Brecht's irreverent and daring re-interpretation of the German classic. "Urfaust is a kind of well-spring for German theatre... The love-story is the most daring and the most profound in German dramatic literature." Brecht

ISBN: 978-0-9534-257-0-9 (1998) €10